*To the people*
*For keeping the faith*

*Perish policy and cunning,*
*Perish all that fear the light*
*Whether losing, whether winning*
*Trust in God, and do the right.*

Norman Macleod, 1812-72.

## Titles by *Langaa* RPCIG

**Francis B. Nyamnjoh**
Stories from Abakwa
Mind Searching
The Disillusioned African
The Convert
Souls Forgotten
Married But Available

**Dibussi Tande**
No Turning Back. Poems of Freedom 1990-1993

**Kangsen Feka Wakai**
Fragmented Melodies

**Ntemfac Ofege**
Namondo. Child of the Water Spirits
Hot Water for the Famous Seven
The Return of Omar
Growing Up
Children of Bethel Street

**Emmanuel Fru Doh**
Not Yet Damascus
The Fire Within
Africa's Political Wastelands: The Bastardization of Cameroon

**Thomas Jing**
Tale of an African Woman

**Peter Wuteh Vakunta**
Grassfields Stories from Cameroon
Green Rape: Poetry for the Environment
Majunga Tok: Poems in Pidgin English
Cry, My Beloved Africa
No Love Lost

**Ba'bila Mutia**
Coils of Mortal Flesh

**Kehbuma Langmia**
Titabet and the Takumbeng

**Victor Elame Musinga**
The Barn
The Tragedy of Mr. No Balance

**Ngessimo Mathe Mutaka**
Building Capacity: Using TEFL and African Languages as Development-oriented Literacy Tools

**Milton Krieger**
Cameroon's Social Democratic Front: Its History and Prospects as an Opposition Political Party, 1990-2011

**Sammy Oke Akombi**
The Raped Amulet
The Woman Who Ate Python
Beware the Drives: Book of Verse

**Susan Nkwentie Nde**
Precipice

**Francis B. Nyamnjoh &
Richard Fonteh Akum**
The Cameroon GCE Crisis: A Test of Anglophone Solidarity

**Joyce Ashuntantang & Dibussi Tande**
Their Champagne Party Will End! Poems in Honor of Bate Besong

**Emmanuel Achu**
Disturbing the Peace

**Rosemary Ekosso**
The House of Falling Women

**Peterkins Manyong**
God the Politician

**George Ngwane**
The Power in the Writer: Collected Essays on Culture, Democracy & Development in Africa

**John Percival**
The 1961 Cameroon Plebiscite: Choice or Betrayal

**Albert Azeyeh**
Réussite scolaire, faillite sociale : généalogie mentale de la crise de l'Afrique noire francophone

**Aloysius Ajab Amin & Jean-Luc Dubois**
Croissance et développement au Cameroun : d'une croissance équilibrée à un développement équitable

**Carlson Anyangwe**
Imperialistic Politics in Cameroun: Resistance & the Inception of the Restoration of the Statehood of Southern Cameroons

**Excel Tse Chinepoh & Ntemfac A.N. Ofege**
The Adventures of Chimangwe

**Bill F. Ndi**
K'Cracy, Trees in the Storm and Other Poems

**Kathryn Toure, Therese Mungah
Shalo Tchombe & Thierry Karsenti**
ICT and Changing Mindsets in Education

**Charles Alobwed'Epie**
The Day God Blinked

**G.D. Nyamndi**
Babi Yar Symphony

**Samuel Ebelle Kingue**
Si Dieu était tout un chacun de nous?

**Ignasio Malizani Jimu**
Urban Appropriation and Transformation : bicycle, taxi and handcart operators in Mzuzu, Malawi

**Justice Nyo' Wakai:**
Under the Broken Scale of Justice: The Law and My Times

# Whether Losing, Whether Winning
## Essays in political realism

G.D. Nyamndi

*Langaa* **Research & Publishing CIG**
*Mankon, Bamenda*

**Publisher:**
*Langaa* RPCIG
(*Langaa* Research & Publishing Common Initiative Group)
P.O. Box 902 Mankon
Bamenda
North West Province
Cameroon
Langaagrp@gmail.com
www.langaapublisher.com

Distributed outside N. America by African Books Collective
orders@africanbookscollective.com
www.africanbookscollective.com

Distributed in N. America by Michigan State University Press
msupress@msu.edu
www.msupress.msu.edu

ISBN:9956-558-52-4

© G.D. Nyamndi 2009
First published 2009

# Contents

| | |
|---|---|
| Preface | *viii* |
| 1. Of our past | *1* |
| 2. The political game | *9* |
| 3. The dual heritage | *11* |
| 4. The political journey | *30* |
| 5. The Social Liberal Congress: genesis and growth | *40* |
| 6. The October 2004 Presidential elections | *62* |
| 7. The National Coalition for Reconciliation and Reconstruction (NCRR) | *67* |

# Preface to the second edition

The first edition of this work appeared in September 2004. It went into very limited circulation, mainly among friends and academic colleagues. The response was warm in many cases, even ecstatic in some. I wish to thank all those who opened their minds to my vision, and especially those who reached back to me with observations and/or encouragement.

Events lose their power to instruct if they are not disseminated. If such events are good happenings, their lessons will remain lost to the public unless they are brought alive by chroniclers. As for bad occurrences, their deterrent powers will not be felt unless they are delivered to society by watchdogs.

Cameroon's story has suffered silence all too often. People of this country write very little, especially about themselves; they read even less, especially things of import to their country. The result is that much of our life as a people, our history, that is, is lost in darkness. To recreate it we often have recourse to the shaky possibilities of memory, or to the subjective dictates of vested interests. There is no definitive history of Cameroon, no authoritative text which sanctions our collective march forward and provides guidance and inspiration.

Public officials, especially those elected into office by the people, are first of all servants and teachers, entrusted with the duty to educate the citizens on the social visions and political options that do, or will, guide their stewardship. Where this is not done, the people are denied the right to judge, and therefore the prerogative to sanction.

And yet it must be said: Cameroon is a tender country both in terms of its age and of the events that have shaped its recent history. Born just some four decades ago, the national triangle cannot claim a place among the older nations of the earth. By every measure, the country is still in its infancy, in that age when falling and rising and falling again and rising again are common features of daily experience. Like a child in its infancy, Cameroon will know moments of turmoil born of administrative clumsiness and political lopsidedness. But when such moments come they should not be taken as inescapable signs of doom. Rather, they should be viewed as sure indications of maturation out of which will arise a steadier, clearer pattern of existence.

Four decades is a short time. Against the background of this temporal brevity, some of Cameroon's achievements can be deemed absolutely breathtaking. As late as 1959 Cameroon was a Trust Territory under United Nations management. On 1 January 1960 its French component became independent. On 11 February 1961 the British Southern Cameroons voted in a UN plebiscite to join the freshly-independent République du Cameroun in a new structure known as the Federal Republic of Cameroon. 1 October 1961 celebrates the birth of this new structure.

Between 11 February 1961 and now, much has happened, some scintillating, some bleak, but all blended into the mortar that gives the national edifice its distinctive texture and character.

A tender thing requires care in its handling. Cameroon is one such thing. The events that form the crossbeams of Cameroonian history have touched the country with diverse fortunes. Two such events stand out by the very dint of the threat they have constituted to national cohesion: the "green revolution" of 1972, and the coup attempt of April 1984. Since the death of the Federal system in 1972, Anglophone Cameroonians have become unsure and insecure, restive and justifiably irritable. Francophone Cameroonians do not need to work themselves into this picture: they did not create it. It is not a social problem between one Cameroonian and his next-door neighbour, but a matter of governance, of political games playing. One has to be an ethnic Anglophone to comprehend this statement. The threats to national unity inherent in the abrupt, calculatedly provocative end to the

Federal system in 1972 are to be taken seriously. Cameroon is a tender country!

The 1984 coup attempt also endangered the peace. Here, too, Anglophone Cameroonians need not bother to work themselves into the picture: they did not create it. Like the 1972 "green revolution", the 1984 coup was a power game, and like the "green revolution" it fathered victims across the playground. These two events make Cameroon a very vulnerable polity. And it will take the best of our nationalistic fibre and statecraft to overcome.

These reflections shine their critical light into as many corners of our national life as possible; but more importantly, they invite each citizen to a similar effort. That way no dark spot will go uncovered, and the cumulative strength of our individual lights will shine away the corrupting forces that all too often bog our take-off. In victory as in defeat, whether losing, whether winning, our commitment to the national cause must be impregnable. I do not see any other road to collective fulfilment.

*G.D. Nyamndi*
Buea,

*To Cameroonians,
the anointed architects of Cameroon's greatness*

# 1

## Of our Past

Our existence makes sense only when understood in terms of where we are from and where we are going. If we do not know where we are from, it remains doubtful whether we will know our way forward.

This where-we-are-from element equates with our birth, both collective and individual, into the scene of life. As for its where-we-are-going-to correlate, it corresponds to growth; that is to say a journey on the scene of life.

A journey implies direction not only to but also from. That is what we mean when we say our life is a duality of action from and to, a dynamics, in other words, of progression. This from-to linear progression contrasts with the on-the-spot existence in which we turn round and round on ourselves *ad infinitum*. In the latter mode of existence, time seems to be frozen in one moment: generations come and go, leaving things very much the way they met them, at times in an even much worse state than they met them. In such cases, even our encounter with other cultures leaves only traces, thin and fragile and outlandish, not foundations for take-off. Such encounters leave only weak traces because our core selves either do not open up to, or are incapable of, accommodating the possibilities for genuine change that these foreign cultures bring along. Could ours be a mentality that is obdurate to change, especially when such change is meant to eliminate negative influences in our lives and create room for progress?

The reflections that follow, therefore, are meant to be a projection into the future, that uncharted province where our hopes and ambitions are lodged, and which also presents a mirror record of today's failures and achievements. Whether or not the things dreamed by these reflections happen under our aegis matters little. If they are worthy of human attention they will find architects in other minds and builders in other hands. What they should strive for, above everything else, is relevance to human life; for all action is vain unless it puts a smile on the face of human existence.

A projection into the future is just a way of returning to the past. Experience, that is to say life, is nourished by the dialectical tension between these two extremes. The future is shaped by the past. That is why to travel into the future we must first return to the past, the better to arm ourselves with the mental and moral strength required for the onward march. Take away the past and there is no future; for, as the saying goes, tomorrow begins today and today began yesterday.

The past occupies an important – I should even say unique – place in the life of any people. If we look closely at the history of the world we will find that societies with a sense of direction, societies that know where they are going, are those that have maintained an unbroken link with their past. This link has not only been there for its own sake. It has provided mooring and bearing, lessons and precepts, so that anyone trusting to it has worked with the confidence that only good guidance procures.

Let us look at the great nations of today, beginning with America. American vision will be muddled without the guiding influence of its Founding Fathers. The spirit of America, that collective mystique without which the ordinary American will not be able to define himself, has come over the years to symbolize the continent's sense of indebtedness to its Forefathers. America is what it is today because somewhere in the past a few people laid the right foundations upon which to build today's greatness. In laying those foundations, those builders did not think of themselves only; in fact, they did not think of themselves at all. Their project sought justification in the future, in the people to come many, many years later, and prompted them to anchor their work on transcendent foundations. The American constitution, for example, has been in existence since 1789. During this time the amendments it has suffered can be counted on the tips of the fingers. That document continues to be the country's single most fundamental text and the repository of its ideals, many, many years after the death of its authors. And precisely because these authors worked for posterity, they have become the timeless custodians of America's condition; they have attained immortality in ways in which no temporary self-indulgence could ever have rewarded them.

Similarly, when the French make proud reference to *nos ancêtres les Gaulois (our ancestors the Gauls)*, they are acknowledging in their own way the salutary link with their ancestors. On the day of François Mitterrand's investiture as President of the French Republic, he marched down the Champs Elysées, alone, rose flower in hand, and in full view of a consenting nation, allowed himself to be swallowed by the Pantheon, there to seek the benediction of his ancestors.

The Pantheon is a monument of great power and dignity built between 1755 and 1792 by the French architect Jacques-Germain Souffot, first as a church, but later transformed into the resting place for great Frenchmen. Voltaire, Jean-Jacques Rousseau, La Fayette, Hugo and Zola are among those buried there, under the inscription, "Aux grands hommes, la Patrie reconnaissante" (To great men, from a grateful Fatherland). It is there in the Pantheon that one of France's greatest Presidents in modern times went to seek spiritual nourishment and political wisdom.

The French are attached to their past in a way that will stir any people to jealousy. If there is anything Cameroonians should copy from the French, it is precisely this attachment to the past. For this to happen we must make our past fit to return to. We must resurrect our heroes, exhume them from their local and foreign places of shameful nightmare, and relocate them in a Pantheon of our making, place of quiet sleep; there for the children of today and tomorrow to come and say: *here they lie, those who built for us!*

The present is but the past extended! There is an unbroken, unbreakable chain of continuity and causality between a people's past and their present. If Germany is one of the most humanitarian nations today on earth, it is because one day in that country's recent past a doctrine was invented and propagated to the effect that human beings were grouped into stocks, some pure, others with blemish; a doctrine that earned the country the opprobrium of the entire world. The German people performed a genuine act of contrition and are today the greater for it. They did not disown that past because of its ugliness. They inherited it, took responsibility for its legacy, and learned the lessons it taught them.

Now, what does the past mean to us Cameroonians? First of all, are we aware of our past in the same way that the Americans or the French or the Germans are aware that they have a past to which they are inseparably bound? Are we conscious of the existence of an unbroken link between us and those who went before us? How far back into our past can we go and still be proud to do so? In other words, is our past the same sacred storehouse that the Western world see theirs to be, or just some opaque province with no practical use to our lives?

The way we react to these interrogations impacts our present lives directly and fundamentally. If we are proud of those who went before us, we will be proud of those who will come after us and as a matter of synthetic harmony we will be proud of ourselves. We cannot place our present against a background of nothingness and hope to make any meaning of it. There is as much value in our present as we extract from our past!

What we call the past remains raw material until we refine it into our history. For this to happen we must as a prerequisite, develop a culture of history writing: a kind of national historiography that makes us understand that history is nothing but events organized for ideological and didactic purposes; and that therefore there are as many historical accounts of the same event as there are ideological positions to defend. History thus refines into the subjective recreation of events based on the overriding interests of the moment. The terrorist/hero dichotomy in the world today stems precisely from this duality of interpretation of the same act. Freedom fighters across the world fall under one or the other category depending on who is looking at them. To the people whose freedom they are fighting for, they are heroes; to those from whom they are struggling to wrench the freedom, they are terrorists.

The German thinker Hegel (1770-1831) tells us that "truth unfolds itself through the course of history, and to obtain knowledge of the world as a cosmic process one can neither begin with axiomatic truths nor can one assume that there were, at one time, primeval people who had been taught by god and were thus endowed with perfect insight and wisdom, possessing a thorough knowledge of all natural laws and spiritual truth." What this statement means is that the whistle in life's race went at the same time for all the peoples; that no race came to the world before the other or was given the secret clues to survival while other races were denied such clues. The myth of the chosen race is therefore to be discarded since it fuels the naïve and defeatist fallacy of one race having had more chances in life than the other races.

We all started life on an equal footing, Blacks and Whites alike. It is even claimed that the Black race had a headstart on the White race since human evolution is traced to the Nile Valley. There is therefore no objective reason why, at the very least, we should not be running neck and neck with the other human groups in the race for supremacy. If we have been out-distanced, out-classed, left behind, we only have ourselves to blame. And if you look round on our continent today you will see just how terrifyingly responsible we are for the myriad catastrophes besieging us; just how ready and happy we are to justify and at times even celebrate famine and genocide where altruism and brotherhood would have done the trick. If Africans loved one another just one-thousandth as much as Europeans loved us, we would be a great continent. Alas! Intra-African love and solidarity is just as refreshing in its abundance as the cool streams of the Sahara.

Now, let us imagine a situation where, at the same time as Europeans were exploring Africa, Africans were exploring Europe and colonizing whole expanses of territory there and subjugating populations to the African way of life. Would Africans too not have experienced and enjoyed the charm of being colonial masters? Would they too not have caused their whips to crack over the sweating heads of white slaves in the cotton fields of Chad and Mali, or the groundnut fields of Senegal and Gambia, or for that matter the timber forests of the Congo basin? The slave trade would have occurred, certainly, but in ways both startling and glorifying to the Black race. Alas! While the White race in all its shades marched on us, propelled by courage and knowledge, we waited, indolent, to deliver a race into bondage then, today, and if care is not taken, for always.

Races, must it be said once again, are not stratified along colour lines but rather along performance indicators. In apartheid South Africa for example, the Japanese were regarded as first-class citizens while their Chinese neighbours were given the same treatment as coloured people. Racially, the Japanese and Chinese belong together, to the yellow race, but in terms of technological advancement, at least in the apartheid days, Japan belonged in the first-world and China to the third-world. However, rather than sit in their distant corner and complain about discrimination against them, the Chinese rose to the challenge in science and technology. The result is there for everyone to see: China is today one of the world's most buoyant nations whose scientific and technological might has been placed at the service of a rapidly expanding economy. Throughout the world, the Chinese are not only respected; they are even dreaded! The Yaounde Conference Centre, the most outstanding architectural work in our nation's capital, is a telling symbol of Chinese thought and ambition. It is just as if Yaounde was built for us by China and not by Cameroon! We have a challenge there: take back our national pride by producing works that celebrate our grandeur and vision.

If a people do not write their own history, others will do it in their place and from the standpoint of their own interests. It is our attitude to history that determines and reveals our self-awareness.

It must be stated, with some dismay, though, that our level of historical consciousness is very low; at any rate, our level of the consciousness of *our own* history. We derive quite some pleasure in reading, teaching, and even writing the history of other nations, especially those with which we have ties of some kind, but the same interest does not inform our attitude to our own history. As a historian myself, I am bewildered at the qualitative and quantitative paucity of material on Cameroonian history. Things go on just as if there was nothing worth writing about on and in Cameroon. We seem to be ashamed of our past! The result is that everyone becomes a historical reality unto himself, each one constructing society's history from the interested standpoint of his own conceited importance.

Our past inspires neither admiration nor respect. That past seems to exist on quicksand, the kind that causes traces to vanish against the least wind. That is why our past is not the object of a sustained historiography. We do not return to it for instruction; we do not celebrate its grandeur either. Where will that grandeur even come from if we live like people who fell from the sky and to whom only the present matters? Because we live like strangers from the sky, we are severed both from the past from which we take nothing and from the future for which we keep nothing. Our dominant worldview therefore becomes one of nothingness, imprisoned as it is in our greedy present. This is our basic plight. Because we have no past, we do not think of the future. We do not leave behind marks that will transcend our existence: we seek immortality not through the indelible acts that we bequeath to humanity but in the trivial things that satisfy our momentary appetites. We are the beginning and end of all things. History begins and ends with us!

As we have already said, history is an ideological weapon. It is therefore a discipline to be handled with care because a people's destiny depends entirely on the historical sense that is given to it. If our historical accounts minimize our past, our children will grow up despising that past and will not feel the urge to return to it for guidance.

We are nothing without our past. As Marx says, "Men make their own history, but they do not make it under circumstances chosen by themselves, but under circumstances directly encountered, given and transmitted from the past. The tradition of all the dead generations weighs like a nightmare on the minds of the living." It is interesting that Marx who was not even an African speaks with the power of African wisdom: the dead are not dead; they are in the trees and the rivers; they are in the fields and in the forests. Great minds who have understood this maxim have, by their acts, enshrined their names in the timeless pages of history, the pages to which we of today and those of tomorrow will forever return for the roots of who we are. Such minds have understood that if you invest in your mortal flesh that investment decays with your mortal flesh; but that if your genius serves mankind, it becomes by that same token immortal.

# 2

## The political game

When we say man is a political animal we are saying that he is an ace player in the survival game.

Like any other game in life, politics is a test of good judgment; of the ability to discern the stakes. People who have succeeded in this intricate game have done so precisely because they have been alert to the inner requirements of this discipline. For politics is a discipline both as practice and idea.

In Cameroon these inner requirements are particularly stringent. This stringency rests on the unique heritage of the present-day Cameroonian society. When Paul Biya says *le Cameroun c'est le Cameroun (Cameroon is Cameroon)*, he is drawing attention to the peculiar aura of the country. This is one statement he has made that will earn him a place in the pages of our history, for it gives us a cryptic image of just who we are: a people of exceptions, of paradoxes, but also, and perhaps especially, a uniquely intelligent people; so intelligent as to become geniuses. And we know how dangerously contiguous genius is to lunacy.

Cameroon is one place where logic does not always have its way, where outcomes are never predictable. Here is a country where foreigners have packed their bags in anticipation of a cataclysm only to turn round and find people going about their usual business in the most serene of moods. In one country the price of bread is raised by 33 cents and the whole country goes up in flames. But in Cameroon the currency is devalued by 100%, followed immediately by a 70% slash in civil service salaries and not a finger is raised. The country tops the chart of the world corruption index one year and is sufficiently comfortable with that performance to repeat the feat the very next year. The country is in some kind of democracy, but the election of its president is done in a one-round ballot. The country is a vastly wealthy triangle, yet its entry into the club of poor, heavily indebted countries is celebrated as a national achievement. Cameroon has the poorest football pitches anywhere in Africa but the richest football fame anywhere on the continent. Each one of us has his own personal record of the paradoxes in which the country is steeped.

People have sought explanations to these paradoxes in varying ways. Some have said Cameroonians are cowards; others that they are indolent; yet others that they are narcissistic. None of these claims seems to tell the whole truth. One thing I have grown to admire in the Cameroonian is his resilient intelligence. Whatever we say, we cannot run away from the fact that Cameroonians are clever people. I really prefer the word intelligent. Just watch what they do in football and you will know that they are not a people to take lightly. In the manner of the geniuses that they are, they make football simple: they deconstruct the game, rid it of its orthodoxy, and turn it into a jamboree of individual artistry. Football is one game that tests intelligence!

Cameroonians are masters at perceiving the stakes in any given situation. They never choose the worst option. However bad the situation is, they always find reason to make it look slightly less bad than it really is. The sky is never totally dark overhead. The Cameroonian always finds a silver lining in it – or puts one there from the depths of his impregnable optimism!

Even natural phenomena bend to the strange ways of the country. Mount Cameroon, West Africa's highest peak, erupts, but the larva billows away from all human settlements. The one-kilometre-wide blazing liquid flows downhill for close to eight kilometres, eating up lush vegetation, but stops a hair's distance short of a hotel complex and within sight of the country's oil refinery. At the end, not one house is buried; nor one body.

# 3

## The dual heritage

This man, the Cameroonian that is, with such a rich array of paradoxes, has a past, even if he spends some of his genius trying to obviate this fact. He has a past as surely as he has a future; for Cameroon lived before him and will outlive him. Those who were are no more; those who are will soon be no more.

Historians of the Cameroonian station know the road the country has travelled since its birth. It is a road that has gone through German rule, Anglo-French trusteeship, federalism, the unitary state, to what is now just the state. Each of these stations on the country's journey into the future has etched a specific mark in its face, so that today one cannot talk about Cameroon without referring to those indelible marks. Any politician who fails to see and respond to these marks also fails in his enterprise as a politician.

### Culture

What then are these distinguishing marks? They are cultural first of all. The culture referred to here is not those time-old practices of our ancestors that are woven into the very fibre of our essence, but the acquired, exogenous imprint of western intrusion into our social consciousness.

Cameroon as we know it today is a bi-cultural construct that combines aspects of French and British culture following the dual tutelage of these powers exercised during the trusteeship years. That is why today French and English are Cameroon's official languages. French is in use in what was formerly the French Cameroons, and English in what was known as the British Southern Cameroons.

This cultural specificity has given rise to two qualifiers: *francophone* and *anglophone*. These qualifiers are not linguistic. They are geo-cultural. They have to do with *roots* buried in a specific *place*. A Francophone is therefore not any Cameroonian who speaks French but rather a Cameroonian whose *roots* are in, or are traceable to, that part of Cameroon east of the Mungo and formerly under French trusteeship. Similarly, an Anglophone is not any Cameroonian who speaks English but that Cameroonian whose roots are planted in, or are traceable to that part of Cameroon west of the Mungo and formerly known as the British Southern Cameroons. By dint of this understanding, one will notice that there are Anglophones who do not understand a word of English, Anglophones whose sole language of communication is French. These are Anglophones born and bred in the Francophone part of the country. Similarly, one will notice that there are Francophones who are totally alien to the French language, born and brought up as they are in the Anglophone part of the country.

This Anglophone/Francophone duality is really the storehouse of our national identity and strength and should be seen and projected as such. This is where the importance of history as an ideological tool becomes paramount. The duality should be understood in complementary terms, not in conflicting opposition. And it is the duty of historians to demonstrate how this is possible. It is they to take us down memory lane and show us how and why we undertook the journey that has taken us to where we are today, and in so doing help us to take full and patriotic responsibility for our past.

The duality referred to above indicates that these two peoples have not always lived together. Reunification is understood as "retrouvailles" (reunion), meaning that there had been "séparation" (distancing) at some point, and that therefore the two components had gone their separate ways for some time. These historical facts must be assumed if we intend to make meaning of our present. Rather than try to hide them or behave as if they never happened, we should strive to come to terms with them and see what strength there is to be derived from the wealth of divergent but essentially complementary experiences that they propose to us; for it must be said that we cannot cause the past to disappear with a wave of the hand.

These divergent experiences return us to the trusteeship mandates traversed by the two territories subsequent upon the seizure of Kamerun from Germany by the Allied Powers and the partitioning of the territory between France and Britain in the Franco-British Declaration of 1919. If the Second World War had not occurred, German Kamerun would most probably never have been split and things like the French Cameroons, the British Southern Cameroons, West Cameroon, East Cameroon, the Federal Republic of Cameroon, the United Republic of Cameroon and other related concepts would not preoccupy us today. But that war was fought and the territory was split. These are facts of history from which we cannot run away. We cannot acknowledge our presence in life and yet behave as if the man and woman who brought us into the world never existed. We are who we are precisely because of the meeting of those two unique, exclusively distinct individuals. We are dealing here with an empirical statement that does not accommodate any amalgam or disfigurement.

French and British colonial policies were not the same, not any more than France and Britain are one. This is a truism. Without delving too far into their characteristic features, we can say in a nutshell that where French colonialism rested on assimilation, English colonialism for its part functioned on the basis of Indirect Rule. According to France's colonial vision, territories either belonging to it or put under its care immediately became an integral part of the larger French empire. Known as French Overseas Territories, these colonies were accorded political and economic prerogatives that gave them a semblance of equality with metropolitan France. The result was that most inhabitants of these colonies considered themselves as Frenchmen more than anything else. They went to France to seek fulfilment and recognition, and the more they identified with French culture the greater was their own sense of achievement. To entertain this illusion of oneness, the French themselves settled and mingled freely in their overseas territories where they kept cultural transmission and transfusion steadily alive, mainly through inter-racial marriages. The sizeable French settler population in the Francophone towns of our country, notably Douala and Yaounde, is a residual indication of this policy; and so too is the huge Cameroonian colony in metropolitan France and the continuing pressure on that country's gates by would-be immigrants even today. New French President Nicolas Sarkozy's policy of "immigration maîtrisée" is intended actually to stem this tide.

The French colonial policy of assimilation is a basic factor in the assessment of post-reunification Cameroon, for it underscores the manner in which the dual heritage has been managed in a context of Francophone cum French dominance of the country. This is an objective remark, not a sentimental complaint! Cameroonians living under French trusteeship have come to espouse the French vision of things, and they have done so with such thorough faith that it becomes difficult for them today to understand why Cameroonians of the former British territory should be seeking to uphold a separate identity and should be so intent on propounding federalist doctrines. The assimilationist mentality of the Francophone perceives in such attitudes nothing but attempts to jeopardize the hard-won principle of national integration. These fears are genuine because federalism is alien to the French system of government. This is an area where both sides of the post-colonial divide have to tread with precaution, discernment and intellectual maturity because, strange as it may sound, both of them are correct in their stances!

As a simple illustration of this claim, let us take our minds back to Canada, the only other country in the world that proposes features akin to those of Cameroon, even if in inverse order. Canada is Anglophone, but one of its Provinces, Quebec, is Francophone. Because the dominant culture in the country is Anglophone, we notice that the federalist set-up of the country is maintained, protected and respected. Proof is that the identity of the Francophone province as a Francophone entity has never been threatened in spite of the obvious and understandable temptations to do so.

In fact, the identity of Francophone Quebec is viewed with such pride that most of the Governors of Canada in the recent past have come from that Province. Just imagine what would have happened if Greater Canada had been Francophone and Quebec Anglophone!

On a visit to Canada in 1968, Charles de Gaule cried out at the top of his voice: "Vive le Québec libre!" (Long live free Quebec!). One just wonders how that same General would have felt if a visiting Italian President to the island of Corsica had screamed at the top of his voice: "Vive la Corse libre!" (Long live free Corsica!). Be that as it may, the Canadian situation shows that colonial policies do affect co-existence in different and sometimes very dramatic ways. By this same logic of ideological identification, it is very likely, not to say certain, that if the British Southern Cameroons had been Francophone and the French Cameroons Anglophone - in other words, if the bigger part of Cameroon had been Anglophone and the smaller part Francophone - the 1961 constitution would still be in force today because the dominant Anglophone culture with its federalist outlook would see to it that the federal character of the agreement remained in force. It's all a matter of colonial ideology. As it turned out, the dominant Francophone culture, with its assimilationist temper, paid only lip service to the 1961 federal constitution which it respected just long enough for the signatories to return to their different stations before the whole thing started being undermined. Explanations and justifications may be found to the 1972 "green revolution", whatever that means, or for that matter to the 1984 constitutional amendment, but the truth remains that these two moments were only logical manifestations of a colonial policy that had no regard for a federal system that was alien to its character. Francophones do not need to be apologetic: they are only being themselves and nothing else!

Contrary to the French, the British treated their colonial populations at arm's length. The beautiful method they devised for dealing with their colonies while at the same time leaving them alone was called Indirect Rule, a system which made it possible for them to conduct business with their colonies through local authorities, chiefs and kings for the most part, without any direct contact with the population. The line was drawn between the two parties, a line that was hardly ever crossed, especially by the colonized people in the direction of their masters. The result was that British colonies did not – and were not encouraged to – feel the same sense of attachment to the Metropolis as their counterparts in French colonies felt towards France. If you look through the former British Southern Cameroons today, you will be hard put to it to discover an Englishman or his descendant who settled here out of love for the place or out of a duty to encourage inter-cultural ties between Cameroon and Britain. Such ties were frowned upon, not to say proscribed. Cameroonians of the former British Southern Cameroons therefore went through the trusteeship years with a strong sense of independence and an equally strong attachment to their local cultural values.

Between 1919 and 1961 when reunification was effected, the British Southern Cameroons and the French East Cameroons lived separately; so separately that one needed a pass to go from one territory to the other. And this went on for forty-two years, not a short time when it comes to acquiring new ways. As we have just seen, the growth of each part was conditioned by the colonial mind at the helm, with its own specific approach to the trusteeship question and ultimately to post-independence Cameroon.

The challenge facing today's Cameroon resides precisely in our readiness to assume this duality. There is nothing inherently wrong in being part of one or the other of these two entities. In fact, if these entities did not exist, we would have to invent them for Cameroon to be what it is: Cameroon. If, as we have said, there is nothing wrong in belonging to one or the other of these composite entities, there is on the other hand everything wrong in treating any one of the entities as if it was an enemy territory occupied by enemy peoples. This is the unfortunate impression that has crystallized over the years and which has considerably retarded the onward march of this potentially attractive country. Some trite and offensive expressions which good sense debars us from using continue to enjoy currency in different corners of the country in testimony to the long road that is still to be travelled to reach real nationhood. And it is a road that must be travelled; for the proper destiny of the country does not lie anywhere but on that road swept clean of retrograde forces.

Cameroonians themselves have sustained this puerile animosity at great cost to national cohesion and progress. They have indulged in a practice of blackmail, slander and spite that in the end has left both parties flat on their faces and the national image bruised. In a country where unity continues to present itself as the most needed commodity, one fails to see a conscious effort to build that unity across the cultural divide. One does not see people being brought together, in a context of genuine recognition of differences, to compute their strengths and invest them in a collective enterprise. What one sees, on the other hand, is a sustained effort at proving to the other that he does not belong. The idea of the country as a nation is still a pipe dream. Internal animosities, driven for the most part by petty tribalism, are still too alive for any sense of nation to take root.

This situation has given rise to considerable ill feeling, especially among the minority Anglophones, so that it becomes necessary to climb into their minds to see the real nature of the malaise.

The first grudge one encounters in the mind of the Anglophone has to do with the passing away of a legacy.

Anglophones complain that their own system, inherited from the British, with its own intrinsic features and mechanisms, has been swept overboard. They have now been left adrift, not knowing exactly who they are. A new, unfamiliar, not to say unfriendly, system has moved in to fill the vacuum and has made of them strangers in their own land. The feeling of alienation is still very strong, even among the younger generation of Anglophone Cameroonians who never had first-hand knowledge of British administration. Here is a recent justification of this point culled from *The Guardian Post* n° 0202 of Monday 3 April 2006:

> Some students of the Government High School Mamfe under the guise of the Southern Cameroons Youth League (SCYL), were last week arrested in the presence of the German Ambassador to Cameroon, and later detained at the Mamfe gendarmerie brigade...the students were arrested for brandishing placards carrying messages of freedom and pro-SCNC slogans...They brandished placards with messages that read: "Our leaders join us fight against occupation and enslavement", "Thank you Mr Minister, but how can enslaved and poor people enjoy these facilities?"

This newspaper article demonstrates the seething bitterness that continues to haunt the psychology of minority Anglophones in the country. That the bitterness is here voiced by children tells of its die-hard pretensions. These sentiments are to be taken seriously by whoever is in control, for they are there, and strongly so; and so long as they remain alive, national unity will continue to be a mirage.

Also linked to this fundamental grudge of alienation is the frustration Anglophones experience in their struggle to gain acceptance by the dominant francophone culture. Anglophones discover that no matter how much French they speak, they continue to be perceived by their Francophone peers as Anglophones, not as bilingual Cameroonians who deserve full and equal consideration. These Anglophones argue further that, whereas they are not recognized as Francophones even if they speak all the French in the world, Francophones with just a smattering of English gain full recognition as Anglophones. The new situation is therefore one in which Anglophones construe the question of identity in Cameroon as determined by geo-historical factors while Francophones view it rather as linguistic, especially when it comes to determining who is an Anglophone.

Two categories of Anglophones therefore exist in Cameroon today. We have on the one hand, *ethnic Anglophones* whose ancestry is rooted in the territory formerly known as the British Southern Cameroons. To these people, the British way of doing things, symbolized by a heightened sense of public good, is the standard yardstick. When you mention the police force, they immediately talk to you about Scotland Yard and Ikeja, about politeness and service. Hospitals to them are not places where people die out of neglect, but health institutions where doctors and nurses (the latter corps operating under the moral sanction of the Nightingale's Oath) dedicate their lives in the service of their community. Schoolchildren without uniforms are unthinkable to them. Basically, objectively, this is the way it was when that part of the country was under British tutelage. No civil servant left his job to travel to Buea for anything. Things have long since changed so that you cannot talk of today's Anglophone Cameroon in terms of yesterday's British Southern Cameroons. Today's Anglophone Cameroonian is a hybrid lost somewhere between the ever-receding beacon of Trusteeship and the looming presence of the new Cameroonian reality.

We also have, on the other hand, *guest Anglophones*. These are people who originate from the former French Cameroons and who have come into contact with the English language either through settlement or education. It will be remembered that independence in French East Cameroons was obtained at the cost of a bloody and sustained struggle during which many, many nationalists were killed and whole villages razed out of existence. People fleeing from the inferno sought - and were given - refuge in the British Southern Cameroons where they have lived ever since, producing healthy offspring who today account for the territory's colourful diversity. These again are historical facts that cannot, must not, be obviated or distorted into something else. Anglophone hospitality in these troubled years and ever since thereafter must be extolled for it made it possible in times of strife for whole generations of francophone Cameroonians to be saved from the folly of extermination! This act of recognition, once again, is the job of historians who owe their country the duty to place things in their proper historical perspective. Acknowledging positive action is not a sign of weakness; quite on the contrary, it is a noble show of integrity. History that fails to admit of basic, inalienable truths does a great disservice to its own cause.

Since reunification, and thanks to the policy of integration, many Francophones have settled in the Anglophone part of the country for reasons other than administrative tours. Most of these people are fascinated by Anglo-Saxon language and culture and the openings they accord to lucrative jobs all over the world.

Today schools west of the Moungo are bursting at their seams with Francophone children whose parents perceive the advantages inherent in having their offspring schooled in the country's both official languages. Et c'est de bonne guerre! after all, in addition to being Francophone, isn't it enough to speak some English to be considered Anglophone as well? And when the jobs come, more often than not requiring proficiency in English, the guest Anglophones will be on hand to take them. And so the ethnic Francophone enjoys his citizenship to the fullest while the ethnic Anglophone suffers the blight of his Anglophoneness to an even fuller degree. Herein lie the roots of the Anglophone problem, objectified in a deep sense of wrong, an abiding sense of neglect, to use the household euphemism. Whereas the ethnic Francophone is acknowledged as a Cameroonian, the ethnic Anglophone is branded as an Anglophone. His being Cameroonian is marginal, even hazy. He cannot flood schools in Francophone Cameroon with his children because it will not serve any useful purpose. They will come out bearing the stigma of their Anglophoneness. Nor can he show off his French proficiency: his roots will render such proficiency useless. An ethnic Francophone can breeze in and out of positions in the Commonwealth Secretariat in London whether or not he speaks — or even understands — English. Reason? He is a Cameroonian and can therefore represent Cameroon anywhere on earth. That is why in London, New York, Washington, Abuja, Ottawa, and indeed in all the top diplomatic missions anywhere in the world, Cameroon's representation is essentially Francophone. At the same time, however, an ethnic Anglophone cannot get anywhere near the Francophonie Headquarters in Paris no matter how much French he speaks. Reason? The Francophonie is for Francophones, not for Anglophones, no matter how much French they speak.

Ethnic Anglophones worry — and with reason — that a time will come not far from now when only Francophones will be Anglophones in Cameroon, a time too when, as it is already the case, only Francophones will be Francophones in Cameroon, if care is not taken! And this care is the duty of the State.

In the meantime, this vexing matter of Anglophone/Francophone relations is tackled in varying ways by the different stakeholders, each according to the dictates of his vested interests. To the majority Francophones the Anglophone problem is the handiwork of a few disgruntled persons whose minds have remained nostalgically enchained to the Anglo-Saxon way of life, a way of life which, they argue further, held no promise of fulfilment for the Southern Cameroonian. That is why the late Premier of East Cameroon, Charles Assale, could boast that at reunification in October 1961 the British Southern Cameroons was a tattered strip of territory inhabited by hunger-stricken people who fell in the open arms of their new Francophone masters with thankful relief. He even claimed that the population of the British Southern Cameroons was so wretched at reunification that alms had to be collected in the French Cameroons to come to its rescue.

Some mainstream Anglophones equally maintain that there is no such thing as an Anglophone problem and then hasten to produce statistics and examples to assail any arguments to the contrary. The consoling fact in this attitude is that it constitutes more of an interested veneer than the bedrock of the conviction it claims to express.

## Numbers

The distinguishing marks in the present Cameroonian situation are also numerical. Anglophones are fewer in numbers than Francophones. The ratio is 1:2. This balance in itself would not be significant in a situation of mutual trust and respect of pacts. But in the absence of these safeguards the law of numbers becomes potent, even ominous. The smaller fraction loses its voice – and therefore its strength. It is no longer a partner; it is a voiceless subject. It cannot make any claims; it cannot stipulate any demands. That is why since the French Cameroons and the British Southern Cameroons merged in 1961, leadership of the country has been the exclusive preserve of the Francophone majority. There is even a general belief, untried though it may be, that an Anglophone cannot be President of Cameroon. The argument sustaining this belief is numerical: Anglophones are a minority component, so they should keep clear of leadership in a country where the majority Francophones have entrenched claims to such leadership. John Fru Ndi's failure to accede to the Presidency of the Republic after the 1992 elections which he is said to have won is a clear illustration of this point. Most people think he was denied the Presidency because of his minority Anglophone origin. But some finer minds think that he lost the Presidency because he was not bi-cultural.

Although some have questioned why Paul Biya who, like Fru Ndi, is monocultural can be accepted as President of Cameroon and Fru Ndi cannot, the simple answer to this query, and one which derives its strength from the rationale of objective thinking, is that what the majority can do and get away with, the minority cannot. What this means in fine is that, because of his majority background, Paul Biya can be – and is – President of Cameroon whether or not Anglophones like it. On the other hand, John Fru Ndi, because of his minority background, cannot be – and was not able to be – President of Cameroon without the express wish of Francophones and the other power brokers. This is nothing to do with emotions. A politician who fails to capture the subtlety in this proposition will fail in his enterprise as a politician; for, in politics, things are not always what they seem. The power play in the country makes it clear that any Anglophone wishing to exercise leadership must as of necessity obtain the sanction of the *larger* Francophone community.

It must be borne in mind that French culture and its derivatives call the shots in Cameroon – at least for now. Take the case of the military. Even when Cameroon was a federal republic the military was Francophone. It continues to be. It is a well-established fact that French is the language of command in the Cameroonian Armed Forces. Even the police force that is called upon to keep the peace among the population is trained almost exclusively in the French language. Cases of Anglophone policemen berating and humiliating Anglophones in the French language, in the English-speaking part of Cameroon, are among some of the many surrealist happenings that animate our daily lives. Very often, and quite erroneously, these ethnic Anglophone policemen are accused of playing the oppressor's game. The truth of the matter is that they don't have much of a choice. Their professional psychology is fed by one language only,

French, and this point is so firmly implanted in their heads that deviating from it becomes to them a treasonable act. Although they are Anglophones, when it comes to their profession, they think only in French or in whatever bit of it they know; which, more often than not, is not very much. Anglophones joining any of these corps are subjected to a new process of acculturation, with its attendant by-products of insecurity and alienation. Quite often, the young Anglophone soldier is assessed not by his talent as a soldier but by his ability to speak or write French. Language deficiency thus translates into professional inefficiency, and so he is left behind or assigned to chores with no immediate bearing on the exciting business of field command. That is why, of the many Generals of the Cameroonian army, only two are ethnic Anglophones.

Nor is the Anglophone soldier alone to endure such martyrdom. His peers in other fields have the same story to tell, stories of failure and rejection, of ridicule and mockery.

Here is a set-piece of the Anglophone condition in Cameroon, culled from *The Herald* newspaper no. 1548 of Monday 6 September 2004, and captioned: *CPDM official frowns at discrimination of Anglophones in admissions into Buea local council school.*

*Charles Mbella Moki, Mayor of Buea and CPDM resource person, has made bold to speak against the marginalisation of Anglophones in admissions into CEFAM, the local government training centre in Buea. But curiously the Mayor's frank talk did not go down well with some CPDM officials who thought the Mayor's comments were an embarrassment to the regime, coming from a CPDM Mayor.*

*Mbella Moki used the occasion of the recent installation of Mathieu Hagbe, a Francophone, as Director of CEFAM to draw the attention of Kouambo Adrien, Minister Delegate to the Ministry of Territorial Administration and Decentralization in charge of Local Councils (to the fact) that Anglophones in general and Bakweri people in particular were disfavoured in the admissions into CEFAM even though the school was located in Buea.*

Mbella Moki's remarks were contained in his welcome address to Kouambo who chaired the event. The outspoken Buea Mayor expressed disappointment that none of the staff of his council duly registered for training in CEFAM had ever been considered when the admission list was published. "We were embarrassed to see that none of our staff was selected," he said, urging the Minister to ensure that Anglophones were admitted in CEFAM.

Although the Mayor's frank talk was welcomed by Anglophones who have always complained of being marginalized in recruitments in professional schools in Cameroon, some CPDM militants felt it was not right for the Mayor who is a CPDM resource person to confront the Minister in public over admission irregularities. "The Mayor has embarrassed the Minister with his complaint. Why did he not meet him in private to discuss it?" questioned a CPDM militant. Although Kouambo looked embarrassed when the mayor read his complaint, he carefully avoided reference to the issue in his own address at the ceremony.

'The Herald' gathered that the yearly admission of a ridiculously small number of Anglophones into CEFAM and ENAP, all in Buea has always angered the Anglophone community whose protests always fall on deaf ears.

Recently for example, 'The Herald' learned that out of some 800 students admitted into ENAP which trains prison personnel, only about 30 of them were Anglophones. So disappointed were some Bakweri CPDM militants that they reportedly alerted the Prime Minister of the dismal situation during the latter's recent private visit to Buea hoping that he would intervene to ensure that Anglophones were at least given proportional admission. Did he intervene?

This article reveals three things. The first is that Anglophones are not given to speaking out. More often than not, they bear their suffering with equanimity. To openly condemn the injustice they suffer is "to make bold", as the article nicely puts it. In other words, the victim of injustice needs courage to complain. And even when he manages to muster such courage, he is expected to exercise decorum in the place and manner in which he lays his complaint. The Mayor is chided by some of his listeners for transgressing this very important matter of etiquette. The injustice is there for all to see, but it can only be condemned, if at all, within the refined secrecy of the Minister's office.

The second thing the article reveals is that even when Anglophones complain, their complaint invariably falls on deaf ears. Mayor Mbella Moki's plea fetches him only the indifference of the (Francophone) Minister and the rebuke of some of his listeners, certainly the Anglophones on whose behalf he thought he was talking! Most Anglophones take such narcissistic pleasure in their condition that seeking to free them from it is often viewed as a treasonable act. They glory in their misery! They have been thrown so far away from normalcy, so very far away from the prerogatives of a full existence, that by the time they feel the tap of a drop on their parched lips they lap it with thankful relief and look unto whoever dropped it as their God. They are not entitled to the full glass of the water of citizenship; only to the sparing drops that keep them hanging expectantly to a scorching existence.

The life of Anglophones is built on favours from the giver, not on rights from the Nation. Mbella Moki Charles remains the active conscience of his people, for he has understood that you cannot be happy as a leader unless those you lead are happy.

Finally, the article tells us that even Anglophone officials are not able to make things happen for their own people. In times of grief, they cannot be looked up to for solace or reparation. These officials do not pay the piper, so they cannot call the tune! In the corridors of the system, there is no Anglophone clout. The odd sprinkling of peripheral Anglophones hanging out there are too busy protecting their manna to think of their people. A Minister – often without portfolio – is pleased to trek to his destitute village to preach the virtues of peace and unalloyed allegiance to the regime just so that his preaching can reach the ears of his employers and maintain him in his position. All too often the personal is (mis)taken for the common!

A Francophone in Cameroon grows up in a system that is essentially his. No adjustments are required of him, no sacrifices. There is no rupture in his cultural growth. He does not suffer any traumatic changes of system and codes. The capital of his country has always been Yaounde. Gendarmes have always been a familiar sight in his towns and villages. Street tree trunks have always been whitewashed. Homes have always been searched without a search warrant. Suspects have always been detained without bail. His currency has always been the CFA franc. Above all, his President has always spoken to him in French. His children never ask him what the Head of State has said because he spoke only in English, or what that actor in the film on Tele speaking that hostile English language is saying. Everything is done to give full meaning to his citizenship.

But if, as we have seen, the ethnic Francophone is at home in his country, the ethnic Anglophone on the other hand has a grave problem coming to terms with the complexity of his status. His life is a permanent quest for an identity. Who is he? Where is he from? What is his real place in this whole tangle called Cameroon? Can he stand up and be counted? If so, by whom? These interrogations lie at the heart of any reach for public office by an ethnic Anglophone, for they spell out in stark terms the challenges that must be faced if such a person intends to fulfil his mission in the service of his people.

These ills are identified and exposed so that avenues for redress can be sought. It serves no useful purpose to claim that they do not exist, or to think that by dismissing them we are in any way helping to assuage their intensity or even to resolve them. Many of them may be the consequence of a misunderstanding that, if cleared, will make for better relations; but we must all acknowledge their existence and then work towards clearing them to make room for a healthier environment.

# Religion

One other crucial factor in the Anglophone condition in Cameroon is religion. Another German thinker, Feuerbach, sees religion as a projected image of man's essential nature. "Religion," he writes, "is the dream of the human mind. But even in dreams we do not find ourselves in emptiness or in heaven, but on earth, in the realm of reality." In other words, religion is but a screen on which our human ambitions and hopes are projected. Events, however great they become, almost always begin as the expression of a personal yearning. In this regard, it is not to be forgotten that the leader of the French Cameroons delegation to the Foumban Talks was *El Hadj* Ahmadou Ahidjo. As his religious title indicates, he was Muslim. It is believed that his father came from the British Northern Cameroons. At the time of the plebiscite, therefore, he had a certain number of priority goals which he hoped to attain with the help of the vote. Topmost among these goals was the regaining of the British Northern Cameroons, the territory with which he had filial connections. To start with, the return of that territory into the Cameroonian fold would consolidate his Cameroonian identity since both his parents would now be demonstrably Cameroonian. Secondly, by opting for reunification, the British Northern Cameroons would strengthen the Muslim North over the Christian South of the country. The British Southern Cameroons was a predominantly Christian region. Its Premier, John Ngu Foncha was a fervent catholic. In fact, his wife founded the Catholic Women's Association, CWA, one of the most successful church groups anywhere in Cameroon today. If the British Southern Cameroons combined its Christian strength with that of the already important Christian population in the French Cameroons, the resultant equation would be too blatantly against the Muslim North. Losing such a religious threat to Nigeria was thus considered by Ahidjo as a welcome blessing. Instead, and much to his dismay, the exact reverse happened: he lost the Muslim British Northern Cameroons to Nigeria only to be saddled with the Christian British Southern Cameroons. To express his grief, he decreed three days of mourning at the publication of the plebiscite results and petitioned the UN over the conduct of the elections in the lost territory. The British Southern Cameroons therefore entered the federation in tears. Those tears are still to be dried. It entered the federation with the flag at half-mast. That flag is yet to fly at full mast.

It is to be imagined that if the leader of the French Cameroons at the time of the plebiscite had been a Bamileke or a Douala, the fortunes of Anglophones would have been less bleak. In fact, the argument Foncha used to impress the reunification option on his people was that they were returning to their brothers. And there was – and still is – sense in what he said. The Bamenda grassfields, his area of origin, bears very close cultural and topographic resemblance to the Bamileke region that lies to the east of its borders. But for the artificial line thrown between them by colonialism, there wouldn't be any obvious reason, cultural or otherwise, not to consider them as one people. As a young student in Sasse College in the 60's, I knew that my Bamileke schoolmates came from a village not far from Kumba, possibly from Tombel!

Further down towards the coastal region, the Sawa clan is said to extend from Douala in Francophone Cameroon to Mamfe in the heart of Anglophone Cameroon. There is no discernible cultural fracture between the Bakweris and the Doualas, so that one begins to wonder what the governing rationale for colonial territorial demarcations was. Be that as it may, and just so that a people's destiny should be fulfilled, *El Hadj* Ahmadou Ahidjo was the Leader of the French Cameroons at the time of the 1961 plebiscite. There is need, one should say, for some of these inherited frustrations to be re-visited and killed. They have outlived their usefulness; to the extent, that is, that they were ever useful at all.

# 4

## The political journey

Up until 1999 I was a member of the *Liberal Democratic Alliance* Party. This Party was born out of a merger between the *National Democratic Party, NDP*, and the *Liberal Democratic Party, LDP*, headed respectively by Hon. Henry Fosung and Mola Njoh Litumbe. But on 1 November of that year I wrote the following letter to the *LDA*'s National President, Mola Njoh Litumbe:

*Your Excellency,*

*I wish by this letter to inform you that I have resigned my position as $4^{th}$ National Vice President of the Liberal Democratic Alliance and as a member of the Party.*

*During the few years of collaborative effort which we shared, we strove, you, myself and a few other committed militants, to give body to the dream of our Party: to make Cameroon a better place not only for the privileged few but for the deserving majority. A few happenings occurred within the Party which made the fulfilment of this mission impossible. I have therefore thought it wise to invest my energy in a more meaningful enterprise.*

*I wish once again to say how thoroughly I enjoyed your partnership. May God bless you and the Liberal Democratic Alliance.*

*Yours sincerely,*
*George Nyamndi*

The few happenings I alluded to in the letter were basically the internecine struggle for leadership of the Party that sacrificed the goals we had come together to pursue and transformed what had begun as a healthy dream into a nasty game of backstabbing and intrigue. I saw in that standoff a scaled-down symptom of the evil that destroys corporate life when personal drives clash with and override the collective good.

The short time I spent in the LDA taught me in very strong terms just how important leadership was to the fortunes of any collective enterprise. The Party was founded on a very attractive mission statement bulwarked by a rich array of talents, but at the end it faltered on just the point that mattered most: leadership. This slip stripped it of its sense of direction, causing it to splinter off into fragile factions that consumed one another until nothing was left.

The precocious death of the LDA bore a close parallel to the very story of the British Southern Cameroons and stressed the crucial importance not only of commanding leadership but also of unity of purpose in a people's collective march forward.

In the days leading up to the fleeting independence of the British Southern Cameroons, the country had to enter into negotiations with the French Cameroons. The theatre of the showdown was Foumban in the Francophone part of the country. At this point already, the French Cameroons had clinched the home advantage: they were in their element and therefore in a stronger position for negotiation. Overwhelmed by a sense of alienation, the British Southern Cameroons negotiators entered that town as strangers. The edge that goes with hosting an event was denied them even though it was *their* future that was on the scale. Why Foumban, one could ask, and not Douala or Bafoussam, or for that matter Buea or Bamenda or Mamfe? Who decided where such a crucial encounter was to hold? What factors did they consider in deciding the venue for the meeting? The journey to Foumban was an initiatory act of estrangement, a kind of journey into exile which was going to be a dominant leitmotif in the Anglophone experience thereafter.

In negotiations, the venue is just as important as the expertise. If you can bring the other party over to your house, you can equally well make it see things your way. And that was just what happened. The negotiators from the British

Southern Cameroons were taken for a ride in Foumban, literally and figuratively, and returned to Buea with their hands and briefcases full of nothing. In retrospect, one realizes that what was on display in Foumban was not so much the astuteness of the French Cameroonian politicians as the gullibility of the British Southern Cameroonian visitors. The latter were dazed by the pomp and magic of the reception in Foumban and mistook the glitter for the gold. Good leadership does not stop at the glitter: it goes for the gold.

It is a sad commentary on the quality of the Southern Cameroons leadership of the time that up to this day no one can say what it brought back from Foumban. And yet we are talking about the destiny of an entire people. The famous document on which reunification was predicated was never taken back to the concerned people, that is to say the people of the British Southern Cameroons, for scrutiny and opinion. So what then were the trade-off terms for reunification; what the guarantees, constitutional and institutional, that signatories would not renege once the deal was sealed? As the saying goes in French, *la confiance n'exclut pas la méfiance!* The Southern Cameroonian negotiators may have had – and certainly did have – confidence; but were they watchful?

Ahmadou Ahidjo for his part came to the rendez-vous armed, as a good leader should, with zeal and zest, and carried home a handsome booty to his triumphant people. Here are the roots of Francophone ascendancy over Anglophones. Contrary to accepted thought, that ascendancy is not propelled by numbers. Numbers are not a qualitative argument, as the Israeli example so eloquently demonstrates. No! That ascendancy is traceable rather to the aura of invincibility that Ahidjo brought to bear on the Foumban Talks and in all the other related transactions ever since thereafter. He could bang his hand on the table and be listened to. Foncha could not. Ahidjo could ram a warped document down the throats of Anglophone negotiators. Foncha could not displace a comma in that document. Ahidjo could decree that the French version of that document was authentic. Foncha could not see, much less say, that such a stance amounted to the outright dismissal of the other language; indeed of the other party to the negotiations! Ahidjo sized Foncha up – and through him the entire British Southern Cameroons – and found him light. Reversing that image has been – and continues to be – the uphill task of the Anglophone consciousness since 1961.

Good leadership! Commanding leadership! This is the clue to all human success. Mankind's history is reducible to the fight for survival. Over the ages, human groupings have survived or perished according to their ability or not to ensure internal cohesion and stem the tide of external attack. A good example of this principle is provided by the Germanic society of the $5^{th}$ century. Its local chieftain organized his following into a *comitatus*, that is to say a structure in which the chieftain provided his retainers, his followers, with their livelihood in exchange for their loyalty and service. This was a period of territorial fluidity, a period in which battles were fought in order to win and consolidate new frontiers.

The Germanic *comitatus* did not choose its leader haphazardly. Great care was taken in the exercise given that the very survival of the group depended on the leadership resources of the chieftain.

Today's world can be viewed as a juxtaposition of *comitatuses* with the same if not greater demands on the quality of leadership. Cameroon as a modern-day *comitatus* requires good leadership, the prime mover of development.

We all know that development is the engine of social progress. To George P. Shultz, the erstwhile U.S. Secretary of State, the real meaning of development is obtained in the well-being, aspirations, dignity, and achievement of each individual. The process of development is fulfilled when every man and woman in a society has the opportunity to realize his or her fullest potential. The fundamental concern of development is therefore human beings and their needs.

Development is thus meaningless at the macro level of society, the state, the nation or other such encompassing formulae, unless it is rooted in the micro, minute soil of individual fulfilment.

George A. Keyworth II, Science Advisor to President Reagan, underscored this point when he said "the study of global issues is the study of people, and the study of people is the study of values." What all of this means is that society receives its credentials from man, and that therefore if man does not achieve, society cannot boast. The organic link between individual ambitions and the societal image thus underpins the primary concerns of development. To quote David Apter,

> Parallels between the lives of human beings and the life of society and the state are emphasized in evolutionary terms. Each is inseparable from the other. Describing how they intertwine under developmental circumstances by identifying key properties of their connections becomes the natural subject matter of developmental politics.

Developmental politics therefore has to do with the choices we operate from among the gamut of possibilities made available to us. And the present world environment does not want for theories. What paradigm the developmental strategies rely on plays a crucial role in shaping the finished product. And here it is necessary to heed George Shultz's caution that context is important because an exaggerated view of problems can lead to mistakes in policy. In other words, if we construe developmental politics as a problem, then our view of the problem must be clear if we do not want to make mistakes in handling it. If we think that Africa is Europe we will make mistakes in policy. If we take Cameroon for Botswana we will bungle our policy choices. Even within Cameroon, if we consider the state as if it was just one tribe writ large, we will punish the state for mistakes of a tribe and see shortcomings where we should be extolling strengths. A proper view of issues is fundamental to our handling of their stakes.

In the Old English poem *Beowulf* we are told that the Danish king Hrothgar was a successful warrior known for his many exploits in battle and his victories over enemy peoples. These victories were objectified in the treasures he brought home and in the gifts he lavished on his retainers. To earn the allegiance and respect of his subjects he played his role of provider and protector to the fullest. In times of adversity he marched in front; in moments of celebration he sat in the centre, giving freely of the booty of war. His followers were not thrown about in distant, unprotected places, abandoned to hunger and misery. No. He built for them a great hall, Heorot, in which they feasted under his watchful and benevolent eyes.

As we can see from the example of the Germanic *comitatus*, the choice of a leader is crucial in the survival strategies of any community. Cameroon as a modern-day polity is no exception. Its fortunes are inextricably bound up with the quality of its leadership. If the leader is hardworking he will instil the work ethic in his people. If he is benevolent he will educate his community in the virtues of kindness and magnanimity. His trustworthiness will impact the way his people relate to money and property. A people's collective image is underpinned by the singular attributes of their leader.

If we agree that leadership is of primary importance in how well or how poorly people fare, then we will also agree that the developmental effort in Cameroon, construed as a qualitative leap forward, must be subsumed in a corresponding leap forward in the quality of its leadership. Care must be taken in this perilous exercise. Only the very best that the time can offer must be accepted. Anybody can be a leader, but not anybody can be a *good* leader. And a good leader is that person who reflects, embodies, articulates the aspirations of his time and place.

In a country like Cameroon, known for its sizzling complexity on account of its dual colonial heritage and myriad tongues, achieving a proper blend of leadership qualities becomes quite a challenge. The question of profile takes on new meaning. Who can lead a country like Cameroon? Who is that person with the qualities capable of capturing the willing loyalty of every Cameroonian? We will not enter into the vain exercise of producing the ideal Cameroonian leader. What we can do on the other hand is etch out some of the attributes of such a leader. To do this we will return to our Old English epic poem *Beowulf* for inspiration.

The hero in the eponymous epic piece *Beowulf* was noted for his bravery. He met dangers head-on, fought with dragons and monsters, swam the raging seas for seven days. This bravery was refined by a solid trust in God. The Almighty preceded and concluded each one of his day, however calm it was, however tumultuous it turned out to be. Beowulf's happiness was never complete unless it was lost in the happiness of his followers. He lived for them so that he could better live for himself. Mention of his name filled his retainers with mirthful joy: they felt loved, protected, even dotted upon. They knew no fear of want for they knew their leader to be provident. Beowulf was the heartbeat of his *comitatus*.

Can Cameroon produce a modern-day Beowulf? If it can, where does it go for him? The answer lies with Cameroonians, for if you know what you want and apply your faculties to its search you end up finding it. Such a leader, such a Beowulf, would issue from a culture whose organic features closely approximate those of the Germanic *comitatus*. The different cultural groupings in Cameroon are each distinguished by specific features. In the one, work is the standard; in the other leisure; and yet in others allegiance to feudal norms. Some cultures dwell on a barn economy, one in which care for tomorrow informs the efforts of today. Such cultures prepare for the hardships of the dry season by a cautious husbandry of the rainy season's abundance. There, waste is anathema: you face exile, a lasting alienation, if, rather than add to the collective store, you deplete it. It is a culture founded on productivity and efficient management.

Like the other aspects of social life, leadership grows out of, is rooted in, the time-old values of a given polity. These values, as we have seen, are not homogeneous. They differ from group to group in consonance with the existential priorities of each group. As Soyinka questions, can anyone really add up: two oranges, three hoes, four traditional healers, two roadside mechanics, and five beaded crowns? The answer to him is not 16. But as he explains, their intrinsic and overt productive processes do offer us an insight into the lived culture of a society. A consumerist culture will not produce goods; it will squander what it meets and then fold its arms waiting for providence. A productive culture will guarantee today's needs and tomorrow's contingencies. All these paradigms obtain in Cameroon. Choosing the right one is the fundamental challenge the entire nation must live up to.

To return to good leadership, the closest the Anglophones ever came to it was with Augustine Ngom Jua. He was Premier of West Cameroon for a painfully short time, but during that time he demonstrated the firmness and determination that were so dismally wanting in his predecessors. Jua was one man who could tell Ahidjo, straight to his face: this is unacceptable to my people! Or: I too can be President of this country! Ahidjo respected him for that; but that respect was tinged with fear. He knew that with a leader like A.N. Jua a people could see their way into greatness. Jua was definitely not the kind to take chances with. No one could put it past him to restore dignity to his people, to free them from their slovenly lot. He had to go. Whether or not he was killed is beside the point. All we know is that he died, and with him went the promise of great leadership and a great future for the people he led.

Seeing the stakes in a given situation: that is the mark of good leadership. Reaching beyond the glitter for the gold:

that is the power of good leadership. The stakes in the Foumban Talks were momentous. Ahidjo knew that. He knew he had some golden rewards to reap and take home – no, hand over to his people since the Talks were holding in his backyard anyway. And so he came prepared, with advisers and tacticians, strategists and prestidigitators, pimps and whores, each one of them in charge of a specific aspect of the Talks. Ahidjo's team had lawyers and soldiers, businessmen and psychologists, all operating under the watchful supervision of tried and interested expatriate expertise.

The French are a different breed of colonialists altogether. Their own brand of colonialism is one that blends well-meaning assimilation and paternalistic egalitarianism. This method stems from their strong belief that while being human, the colonized man cannot quite be trusted upon to stand on his own feet. For this reason the master is never too far off. He never quite lets go of his colony. Maybe the benevolent humanism that makes him dream of a day when the colonized and the colonizer will communion as equals also forbids him to abandon the field of his experimentation altogether. He is aided in this by the readiness of the colonized to accept and proclaim their subservience, mostly through overt acts of allegiance performed to the accompaniment of puerile sycophancy.

The French did not abandon Ahidjo. Such an act would have defied the norms of their colonial ideology. Their controlling presence made him strong and confident and provided him with the necessary fillip for negotiations.

Foncha for his own part was not so blessed. Whatever criticism he may come in for, it must be acknowledged, in all fairness, that the British habit of quick and total pull-out did not help him very much. Not one single British man stayed behind once the Union Jack was lowered at the end of their trusteeship mandate. They scurried off, leaving behind only corrugated makeshift barracks as testimony of their fleeting presence on Cameroonian soil.

One thing about the British is their sense of respect for principles. They were given the Southern Cameroons to hold on trust for the United Nations. When the latter asked for its territory back, they handed it back, as it was given to them. At no point did they try to transform a trusteeship into a colony. Because they knew that the Southern Cameroons was not their colony, they did not undertake any development projects in it. They did not even bother to know how rich the territory was. That is why Mr Allan Lennox-Boyd, the Secretary of State for Colonies could brazenly tell Foncha at the Lancaster Talks that the British Southern Cameroons was too poor to stand on its own; that the British economy was not there to prop lame territories; and that the keys of the Bank of England would not be handed over to him if he stuck to his plans to secede from Nigeria. History is replete with such ironies.

Foncha was alone in his war with Ahidjo. No amount of goodwill on his part could have rescued him from the planned deluge. With limited education, limited exposure to world events, and aided on by nothing but an odd array of brave companions, he must have been more of a curiosity in Foumban than anything else. Ultimately, the story of the British Southern Cameroons is one of shipwreck subsequent on the captains jumping ship in the stormy seas of nation building. Entering national politics from such a background requires tact and foresight, for the prejudices are many, the stereotypes formidable.

# 5

## The Social Liberal Congress: genesis and growth

Another thing I said in my letter to the National President of the Liberal Democratic Alliance was that I was going to invest my energy in a more meaningful enterprise. The confluence of energy and enterprise amounted to a grand design which I spent the next one year mapping out.

Although I officially resigned from the LDA in 1999, I had in actual fact called it quits with that Party as far back as 1996 when it became clear to me that the leadership struggle at its helm would ineluctably destroy it.

During the ensuing four years, between 1996 and 2000, I spent time with some close friends dissecting Cameroon. One such friend was Albert Azeyeh, Professor of French at the University of Buea. He and I would sit for long hours in El Dorado, a bar on Molyko's busy street, absorbing lively gulps of the Cameroonian quagmire.

Either because of the metaphoric charm of its name or on account of its handiness, El Dorado held for us a fascination whose power lay beyond alcohol. Beer was a pretext, politics the pursuit. We discussed Cameroon, its economy, its democratic experience, its place on the world scene; above all, we sought insights into the steady decline in moral values and how this decline told on our collective destiny.

As an indication of the decayed state of things, Cameroon had been rated the world's most corrupt country for two years running, from 1998 to 99. This was more shame than most Cameroonians could take, but embarrassingly enough, the state itself was unremorseful. One expected to see the regime clutch its face in shame. Instead, one was treated to a surrealistic spectacle of official protests and even threats against the authors of the ratings. The fact that Cameroon was corrupt did not seem to be anything to worry about, only the glamour of its rating. In fact when the country moved from top to sixth place two years later, the matter was celebrated with thorough frenzy, as if to say at least we could now point up above at five bigger ruffians than us!

As our nightly meetings at El Dorado multiplied, it became clearer to us that a collective therapy was required for the country. Each of us had his own idea of what such a therapy would be. My friend saw it in an NGO with an educative thrust; I, in political revival. Cameroon could yet get back its lost dignity if a new political roadmap was designed for it. That was the project I embarked upon and which culminated in the founding of the *Social Liberal Congress* and its legalization on 13 June 2000. I invited Professor Azeyeh to join me in the venture as Secretary General and was pleased when he accepted the invitation. He is an intelligent man with an astounding power of analysis. Other friends joined the pioneer team, namely Zachary Nsutebu as Political Secretary, Ngu Peter Mbavuwa as Treasurer, and Yuh Francis as Organising Secretary. All these persons were my friends and each one joined my political venture out of belief in that friendship.

Whereas I could trace and control the path of this friendship with most of them, when it came to Ngu Peter Mbavuwa a certain urgency overwhelmed the relationship. My meetings with him were always attended by a sense of foreboding, of a faint bell tolling. He died on 13 March 2004 of prostate cancer. I continue to be thankful to him for having offered his elegant Toyota Land Cruiser to convey me to the launching of the Party on 1 December 2000. The alternative would have been to trek to the rally grounds or then alight from my crumbling 504 if ever it survived the 2-kilometre journey from my Upper Bonduma residence to the Molyko Stadium.

But the legacy for which the Party will forever remain indebted to Ni Peter is belief in our purpose. As I said in my tribute to him, "You had faith in your people and conviction in their ability to lift themselves out of suffering. You have taken leave, but I know you are closer to us now than ever before, for you are by Him who causes all things to happen, in the first instance. Your transition is a symbol of things to come. In your death we see the end of a people's plight. In your new home we behold the place of justice and love, virtues in the pursuit of which you dedicated your whole life."

The *Social Liberal Congress* was launched on 1 December 2000 at the Molyko Sports Stadium. As I addressed the fair crowd on that day I knew that my words reached beyond the listening ears and journeyed far, far, into the Cameroonian hinterland, there to throw the basis for a new spirit. I talked against a blue sky to applause whose wealth surprised me both in its spontaneity and its sincerity. Maybe my listeners were rewarding my own candour which rang out distinctly as I bellowed from the lectern, all done up in a marine-blue suit, a gift from my friend and classmate, Jacob Agbor. He'd flown the material in from South Africa; he was later to learn that my political mentor was Nelson Mandela.

Because I write my speeches myself, they say a lot about my psyche. The one on that afternoon of 1 December 2000, produced here-below in its entirety, was short, as my speeches tend to be, but it visited interesting compartments of my political thinking, especially at a time when the country was experimenting with political pluralism.

> *Representatives of Friendly Political Parties*
> *Citizens of the Social Liberal Congress*
> *Fellow Cameroonians*
>
> *In accepting his nomination as Democratic candidate for the Presidency of the United States of America in 1960, John Fitzgerald Kennedy told his countrymen: "We stand on the edge of a new frontier." Those words marked a new beginning for America. They marked a departure from a past of despair and disillusionment to a future of hope and promise.*

*John Fitzgerald Kennedy was a great man. And so I have turned to him for inspiration.*

*Fellow Cameroonians,
Dear Countrymen,*

*Today we stand on the edge of a new frontier. On this day Friday 1 December 2000 a new dawn has broken on our country: a dawn pregnant with hope, a dawn loaded with sunshine. And it is the duty of the Social Liberal Congress to translate those hopes, those aspirations, into reality. It is a historic mission and one that, God willing, we shall perform to the satisfaction of all. I stand here today to make this solemn pledge in the name of the Party, a pledge that is a mark of our genuine commitment to the fortunes of the Cameroonian nation.*

*My Dear Countrymen,*

*The young Party whose first official outing you are witnessing today is conscious of the historic role that destiny has bestowed upon it. It is a historic role that demands courage, wisdom, commitment, but more especially humility and benevolence. For these reasons, the Social Liberal Congress shall have the duty to raise politics to an art, an art sustained by the permanent quest for brotherhood, understanding and progress. In this young Party we dream of a time when politics will no longer be a nightmare but a pleasure, of a time when politics will become the bridge to a future in which Cameroonians, all Cameroonians, walk tall and proud, as the chosen children of a God-blessed country.*

*For indeed, My Dear Brothers and Sisters, Cameroon is not elsewhere. It is here. It is now. It is us. We are Cameroon! Such is the verdict of our collective destiny. None of us present here today, or anywhere else in this country, chose to be born where we are. No Anglophone chose to be born Anglophone in a predominantly Francophone country. No Francophone chose to be born Francophone in a predominantly Anglophone world environment.*

No Cameroonian chose to be born black in a world controlled by white culture and technology. But here we are, Cameroonians, all of us. We belong together. We are destined to remain together. And because our destinies are linked together inseparably, we owe a duty to all the sons and daughters of this country to make our lives as Cameroonians a happy one. We have the power and the means to do so. And do so we will! But we will not do so by driving the sword of division into our hearts. We will not do so by pitting brother against brother, sister against sister, Anglophone against Francophone, South Westerner against North Westerner. We will not do so by preaching the demonic sermon of sons and daughters of the soil on the one hand, and settlers on the other.

My Dear Brothers and Sisters,

Division does not pay. Division has never paid. No country on earth, now or in the past, has ever prospered down the destructive road of division.

A country is like the human body: you cannot cut off one of its organs, however small, and it continues to enjoy full health. No! Like a healthy person who keeps all his organs together, a healthy country must also keep all its sons and daughters together. It must protect them, protect them morning afternoon and evening, like the proverbial jealous parent. Let one Cameroonian fall sick and Cameroon is sick. Let one Cameroonian die and part of Cameroon is dead. For what will Cameroon be without Cameroonians? Cameroon is all we have. Take away from us the pride of being Cameroonians and you have killed us. I say this as one person who loves his country passionately. We all love our country passionately. I see it everyday. Everyday I see Cameroonians suffer in silence. Everyday, yes, everyday, I see Cameroonians die in silence. No sacrifice is too big for them in the name of their country.

Many times I have been moved beyond measure by the sheer fortitude of the Cameroonian. Many times I have marvelled at the fathomless, at times even suicidal love the Cameroonian has for his country. Many times I have been moved. And because I have been moved, I have grown to love and respect my fellow Cameroonians, for that is all I can give them: love, respect, admiration.

My Dear Countrymen,

Because I love, admire and respect you all, I fail to understand why anybody should want to bring you to grief. And yet such is the wanton design of many in positions of influence. Our society is crippled by hatred. This hatred manifests itself in all the insidious forms imaginable. Today in our country it is your province of origin, your tribe, your family that determine your social and professional fortunes. Talent and expertise are systematically swept under the carpet. These practices amount to cleansing. Professional exclusion is an even graver form of ethnic cleansing. We must fight it with the last jot of our blood. Ethnic cleansing has never built any country anywhere in human history. It will not build Cameroon! It can only destroy it. Any Cameroonian worthy of the name must fight the evil of exclusion. We must fight it because its life is our death, its survival our decay.

Fellow Cameroonians,

Great people attain immortality through their legacy to mankind. One such great man was Nnamdi Azikiwe, the venerable first President of the Federal Republic of Nigeria. I wish here to borrow a leaf off President Azikiwe's sixteen canons of rectitude in public life. Basic among these canons were the following:

> We shall not mislead the innocent
> We shall expose and excoriate evil in any shape or form
> We shall be constructive in all we say or do
> We shall resist injustice with all our might
> We shall commend and not discredit merited achievement
> We shall serve without hope of gain
> We shall willingly surrender the reins of office in the usual democratic manner.

*The liberal spirit of these canons shall be manifest in the life and functions of the Social Liberal Congress. In our search for unity and a sense of nationhood, we shall endeavour at all times and in all places to fix the hills-and-rivers fact of the new entity on the imagination of the people.*

*In a country like ours where the enormity of size and cultural density has often militated against national cohesion, our dream of unity must drive us to the task of patient and systematic construction. We shall do this by blending the cultural and linguistic realities of our country into one indivisible mosaic. We shall also do this by transforming our tribal and religious diversity into a new force. We shall extol the virtues inherent in our differences; for it must be remembered: there is nothing like reference to the realities of geography, nothing like respect for the indelible truths of history, to forge a great destiny for a people bonded together by a common heritage.*

*Cameroon is a composite reality of geography, culture and history. Because this is so, we recognize the singular place of Buea, the historic capital of the original, German Kamerun, in the past, present and future of our country. That our Party is born in such a historic setting is no accident of detail. This birth is meant to underline the indispensable role of our history in what we become tomorrow. We will not be doing justice to our country if we fail to recognize that the Cameroon of today was born out of a union of two independent states: the British Southern Cameroons and French Cameroons. We will be failing in our duty to this nation if, for whatever reason, we do not recognize that freedom, independence and equality are the cornerstones of any meaningful effort at nation-building. These principles are inviolate. And so I tell you that if there are ten million Francophones in this country, there are five million Anglophones. That is to say one third of this nation is Anglophone. This ratio must be reflected in every aspect of national life. It is not a favour anybody is asking. It is a God-given right!*

*History has not been kind to us. But then, thank God history has a way all its own of correcting its mistakes. Something tells me, deep inside me, that the time has come. Now is the time for this country to rise to the embrace of its Anglophone children as the intrinsic offspring of a common fatherland.*

*Let me end my address by reiterating this one, permanent fact: Cameroon belongs to Cameroonians, not to Francophones or Anglophones, not to Betis or Bakweris, much less to Sawas and Balis. All these tribes are branches of the mother Cameroonian tree. It is our duty, we in the Social Liberal Congress, you as nationalist Cameroonians, to ensure that our mother tree Cameroon lives on forever, healthy, tall and proud.*

*Long live the Social Liberal Congress*
*Long live Cameroon*

*Thank you and God bless you.*

I looked into the eyes of my listeners on my way down from the rostrum. They were all lit, even ecstatic. Could I have struck the right chord? It looked as if I had. From the market of exhilarating reviews, one segment of the speech seemed to enjoy acclaim: *Cameroon is not elsewhere. It is here. It is now. It is us. We are Cameroon.* I was gratified that those listening to me had read my mind correctly. The emphatic passion of this claim epitomizes my entire political philosophy which is fed by my belief in the total appropriation of existence, in being the thing itself. I had observed not without alarm that the idea of a country as a home was foreign to the Cameroonian official imagination. Quite often administrators of the public estate behaved as if Cameroon was a no-man's land where anybody could collect just what he wanted and walk away gleefully. One lived numbed by this eerie feeling that the nation's safe had been flung open, the natural resources abandoned to the first plunderer, the progeny neglected, the tattered moral fabric at full mast and flapping there in the wind for everyone to see. The paradox of multi-billionaire civil servants in this wretched landscape continues to be one of the most confounding challenges to all good sense; as is Cameroon's triumphant presence in the scum of poor, heavily indebted countries.

The events of 1 December 2000 came after a spate of press interviews to which the birth of the *Social Liberal Congress* had given rise. Cameroon has a fine crop of journalists who can be trusted to mine information from any depth. Clovis Atatah of *The Post* newspaper is one such journalist. The following interview with him on 4 September 2000 gave me the opportunity to clarify some important issues relating to ideology and strategy.

***The Post: Why create a political party now, when we already have more than 120 parties in the country?***

*The problem of politics in Cameroon is not numerical. It is qualitative. We want to place our presence on the political landscape at a qualitative level. The number of existing parties is of no importance.*

***Across the political spectrum, you see political parties virtually running the ideological gamut. Many share ideals. Why did you not join one of these parties rather than create a new one?***

*There is a difference drowning one's voice in a sea of voices and*
*standing out distinctly. It is true that the political landscape is today full of voices singing the same song. But we should be able to perceive the difference between just singing a song and actually translating the words of that song into concrete action. Among the other voices our voice will be the voice of concrete action, the voice of pragmatism, the voice that addresses issues which are relevant to society.*

***Why did you choose the words Social, Liberal, and Congress to constitute the name of the party?***

*Social because we need to address the basic problems which society faces. The desired end result of all political activity is of course social betterment, social improvement.*

*But then, you cannot address social issues with your empty hands. You need the means, and the means will be provided by the liberal imagination, that imagination which feeds all creative endeavours, that imagination that makes it possible for society to produce money. Once your money is produced, you can use it in a more pragmatic, more meaningful way.*

*Now, finally, Congress because we want to put in place a structure which is more like a family; a structure in which members sit round a table and discuss problems of common interest to the family and reach decisions which are satisfactory to as many members of the family as possible. It is a place of debate and consensus, a place of analysis and practical solutions to practical problems.*

**If you want to give a tag to your political party, will you call it a radical opposition party, a conservative opposition, or a party sympathetic to the ruling party?**

*It is still too early in the day to determine where we stand on the political spectrum. However, if you look at our Manifesto and especially at the name of the Party, if you look at our Motto which is Work, Justice, Progress, you will notice that our concern is to go straight to society, straight to the citizen. If in the course of doing this we meet on our way certain views which are like ours, fine. But our Party is not there to look like. We are there to be ourselves.*

**Is there currently any political party in the country which you are comfortable with, vis-à-vis the ideology and the way they operate?**

*Definitely! We are not reinventing the wheel. There is nothing we are saying that has not been said before. The difference is our clarity of purpose, our intentions, and the determination we put in translating those intentions into concrete action.*

*On the Cameroonian political landscape, there has been a clear dislocation between discourse and action. Quite a few political parties have done some good things, but many have failed. We want to improve on the good things that have been done and to correct the mistakes that have been made.*

**When one looks at your current executive, the impression is that it is made up essentially of academics.**

*I'm glad you say that it is an impression. The impression is one that needs to be corrected. It is true that the President and the Secretary General of the Party are university lecturers. But the rest are not. We want an executive that is as representative of social values as possible. The present executive is a skeleton. It has five members only. As the Party grows, so too will the executive become more representative.*

**When did you conceive the idea of this Party?**

*The idea has been in me since I came to Buea in 1993. I have watched the political evolution of the country since 1990. I was saddened by the stalemate which the political process ran into. I therefore thought that the time had come for us to introduce a new vision into what has become a stale landscape. We need a new landscape, a new way of doing things, a new vision that addresses issues meaningfully.*

**The municipal elections are expected in January 2001. Is the Social Liberal Congress going to participate in the elections?**

*No. The birth of the Party has not been made to coincide with any elections. The Social Liberal Congress is still too young. It needs time to acquire the experience that comes with growth; to make itself known to the public.*

*How much time do you give yourself to mature to the point of participating in national elections?*

Given the pace at which things are going, I'd say in six months we should have covered considerable grounds. The Party is moving at a very fast speed. In six months the Social Liberal Congress should become a household name. And, at that point, we shall naturally enter the race.

*Since the Party was authorized, have you had any reactions from the public?*

Yes! The reactions have been tremendous. The people are expectant. There is a general sense of defeat, a sense of loss which is very strong in the population. Visions have darkened. Citizens have been left in the middle of the road, as it were. They have welcomed the Social Liberal Congress enthusiastically. I see this enthusiasm as an expression of the new hope represented by the Social Liberal Congress.

*Would you describe the Social Liberal Congress as a regional or national party?*

National Party.

*Do you already have card-carrying members?*

No, no! We've just finished the party emblem. The next step will be to publish the party constitution, design a party card. Citizens are already yearning for party cards. Not long from now party cards will be available, as well as other gadgets like party caps, pens, scarves, handkerchiefs, you name them.

*Do you intend to do an official launching?*

Yes. We will launch in Molyko, Buea, the Headquarters of the Party. Once that is done, we will move out into the country and launch in other places. The places where we launch will now become the focal *points around which members of the Party in those individual regions will group themselves.*

### Do you have a tentative date for the launching?

*No. It is too early. Right now we are busy with the groundwork, busy with planting our seeds.*

### What is the stance of your party on what is generally known as the Anglophone problem?

*There is a problem. Our Party's stance on this is clear. There are problems that need to be addressed, meaningfully, within the national context. We want to address that problem within the Cameroonian nation. Cameroon does not belong to Francophones any more than it belongs to Anglophones!*

### It is generally understood that to run a political party requires a lot of money. Do you have the resources?

*It depends on what you mean by resources. If by that you mean money, no, we don't have much of it for now. But a good product always finds a buyer. We know that the Social Liberal Congress is a good product, and before long people will be scrambling for it.*

### In a nutshell, how do you assess the performance of the CPDM regime?

*One credit which you must give to the CPDM is that of having held the edifice together during a very stormy period in Cameroon's history. In doing so, of course, it has sacrificed certain priorities. Those sacrifices have in turn weakened the foundation of the edifice.*
*I think the time has come for that foundation to be revisited by other hands and heads so that what was yesterday a weak house can today become a strong, impregnable monument.*

\* \* \*

The main thrust of this interview was the ideological concept of social liberalism which until our arrival was unknown to the Cameroonian political register. As I said in the interview, this concept combines production and consumption, in that order, the underlying argument being that to consume you must first produce, and that, ultimately, you cannot, should not, consume what you have not produced. This does not mean, though, that because you do not produce planes, for instance, you should not acquire them. No. It means rather that the money you use to acquire the planes should be seen to have been *produced* by you. In like manner, you cannot tackle social issues with your bare pockets. Health, education, housing, etc., these concerns are capital intensive by their very nature. No amount of wishful thinking will build hospitals, roads, and schools and provide communities with potable water. Only money will do the trick. It will not do to say we want a hospital built in this village or town and then run to donor countries cap in hand. But it will make all the sense in the world to produce money and then use it to provide the social amenities needed by our different communities.

There are two concepts which the *Social Liberal Congress* does not spend time on. These are *peace* and *democracy*. For anyone familiar with political life in Cameroon, these two notions have worn so thin as to become almost risible. Ordinarily, peace is a state of inner felicity. It is the one thing in life you don't talk about because you are too busy enjoying. When you are at peace you *feel* it; you *know* it. You do not need to be told about it by someone else. Peace is the thing itself: *peace*. It is not a discourse. It comes when every other thing else has been taken care of. And its only known vector is justice. There can be no peace in the absence of justice. Justice is the oxygen of peace! Peace is the reward, justice the effort; one the dividend, the other the investment. If you do not sow justice, you can never harvest peace. And we know that there are no alloys of justice.

Like peace, democracy is action, not talk. Experience has shown that the more you talk about democracy, the less you tend to practise it. To cite Wole Soyinka, a tigre does not need to show off its tigritude. You tell a tigre when you see one! Similarly, you tell a democracy when you see one. A system that spends time theorizing on democracy is suspect. And just like justice, democracy knows no other forms outside itself, no alloys. Advanced democracy is *not* democracy; appeased democracy (whatever that means) is *not* democracy. These artful concoctions are a negation of the thing itself: democratic practice. That is why elections which are the hallmark of democracy are anathema to them. And yet elections are to democracy what justice is to peace. A system that appoints government delegates over elected municipal officials stabs democracy in the chest. A system that disenfranchises citizens stabs democracy in the chest. A system that stifles free expression stabs democracy in the chest.

We are quick to talk of Cameroonian democracy when it comes to our political survival, but never of Cameroonian hospitals when it comes to our health, Cameroonian planes when it comes to flying, Cameroonian designs when it comes to our suits, or Cameroonian palmwine when it comes to our drinks. Much of our trouble issues from this divorce between what we profess and what we practise, what we recommend for society and our own individual indulgences.

*Peace* and *democracy* are the ultimate stages of social and political evolution. They constitute the sacred ideals which the *Social Liberal Congress* is pursuing. And precisely for this reason, they are not amenable to pollution.

The logical corollary of liberalism is work. That is why the motto of the *SLC* gives it pride of place. Work as the defining requirement for meaningful development was the object of another major interview I granted to the intrepid Effa Tambenkongho, still of *The Post* newspaper, on 25 April 2003, and which I have pleasure in reproducing here.

In her preamble to the interview, Miss Tambenkongho wrote: *"Most of the country's political parties are known to parade bogus concepts such as peace, equal opportunities and justice as the centrepiece of their raison d'être. Practically none of them thought it could conceptualize a good or credible work ethic as its motto, until the Social Liberal Congress, SLC, was born, some two years ago."*

**The Post:** *You are known to insist on work as a value Cameroonians should adopt, for all other things to fall in place. Why work and how do they go about it?*

Dr. Nyamndi: Promises are out of tune with the expectations of the electorate. Rather than make promises, you should make the electorate see what the challenges are and make it possible, through pragmatic guidelines, for that electorate to achieve goals which it sets for itself. No politician can set goals for the nation. The nation sets goals for itself and you come in as a facilitator. Yes, what kind of work do we have in mind? Work in its fullest reach: intellectual work, physical work, industrial work, cultural work, etc. We are not going to limit ourselves to certain areas but we will look at work from a comprehensive standpoint, which means that everywhere that a Cameroonian is present, we expect to see him working for his nation, for his own betterment; because what the Cameroonian becomes tomorrow will not be the result of some idle speculation but the concrete result of how much energy he would have exerted to make his own situation better.

*Cameroonians now are so concerned about money. They want somebody who will guarantee them this money. They want to touch. How do you intend to rally them behind your Party?*

The Social Liberal Congress does not make promises: it awakens people to the exciting challenges that lie before them. We are not going to say: here we come with bags of money, or, that is the tree, go there and harvest money. We are going to get Cameroonians unto the road to progress by showing them that the road to progress is not filled with gold which they can bend and pick. It is a road that requires commitment, hard work, steadfastness in their belief in their nation, which can be built on the ethic of work only. Cameroonians are going to have to throw away this destructive concept of access to easy wealth. It doesn't exist. Wealth has to be worked for. And then, within a structure of justice, we share the wealth out so that everybody can have his own share.

**How do you intend to penetrate the Francophone Provinces with the goals and missions of the Party?**

Penetrating other Provinces sounds to me like what is good for the Anglophone is not good for the Francophone. No. We are not dwelling here at the level of geographical or even colonial differences. We are dealing with basic ethical concepts, which are valid, everywhere, and for everybody. Work remains work, whether for Francophones or for Anglophones. We do not need any special effort to penetrate our country because you know that after more than 40 years of coexistence that divide is becoming more and more artificial.

**So far, has the Party extended to other parts of the country?**

We are not talking in terms of Provinces; we are talking in terms of the national territory. The work ethic is alive in every corner of the Nation. Work is one of the key concepts of our national motto which says: Peace, Work, Fatherland. In that respect the Social Liberal Congress is not reinventing the wheel. We are simply highlighting the need for a work ethic as the only way forward in our developmental effort.

**Knowing that the 2004 election is not far away, and that your Party is still to be known, what are you doing about this?**

To say that since the inception of the Social Liberal Congress in 2000 the Party has remained rather discreet is to misrepresent the great efforts that the Party has made towards broadening its base in the country. Now, the Party is very popular. We are not noisy. We do quiet groundwork. You will discover that although people do not come out openly and say the Social Liberal Congress is alive, practically everybody knows that it is. We have taken part in national activities; the Party has marched on National Days. We intend to broaden and consolidate our presence on the ground, especially in the run-up to the Presidential elections.

**What makes you think that you can be the President of Cameroon?**

I think it is the right of every political leader to aspire to the high office of President of the country. Whether you can become one or not is another matter altogether. Once you know that you enjoy that inalienable right, you now work towards its coming true, and that is where the most difficult part of it lies. It is not an impossibility.

**Looking at Cameroonians, it is as if they have nowhere to have their hopes in terms of a new personality. They need a charismatic leader. Can you guarantee them this?**

In all humility, let me say charisma is not an item you pick up from the market. The people know a charismatic leader when they see one. And very often, humility forbids that you lay claim to charisma. It is a very dangerous thing to do because once you give yourself the feeling that you are a charismatic person, you begin to dream dreams which at times lie beyond your own possibility. Let the people proclaim you. Do not proclaim yourself.

**As a Southern Cameroonian, how would you solve their problem if you were voted President of this country?**

Let me make a fundamental correction. I am not a Southern Cameroonian. I am a Cameroonian. It is true that if we go back in history, we will discover that there was a time when Cameroon was made up of two entities. But now, in 2004, it will be politically dangerous to make reference to Southern Cameroons. This does not mean that the cause for which the SCNC is fighting is not a good one. But that cause can find a meaningful resolution within the Cameroonian context if all the key issues are properly addressed. The SCNC cause is not the only cause in Cameroon now. There are other causes, so the simple fact that we are from the English-speaking part of Cameroon does not mean that our Presidency will limit itself only to solving the problems of Anglophones. If you are a national President, your views should also be national: you should seek solutions to problems wherever they arise. We will address the SCNC plea the same way we will address problems from other parts of the country.

**How about problems of unemployment, economic crisis and so on?**

The problems you make reference to are the visible effects of a cause which lies in a structural problem. Cameroon as it is today can only produce unemployment and insecurity because the structure in place no longer guarantees a new take-off of society. In an environment where joblessness is the keyword, it has a spill-off effect. Joblessness means no buying power, reduction in production; it means the close-down of enterprises, especially small and medium size ones. The vicious circle can only be reversed with the coming of a new structure that encourages and attracts investment. Investors like a credible, conducive environment. If there are no investments, there are no jobs. We need a new structure. Once it comes and the international community approves of it, the investors will come, tourism and small and medium size enterprises will boom, jobs will be created, the purchasing power of Cameroonians will be consolidated, and then our society will take off differently. It is up to Cameroonians to provide enabling circumstances for the new society to come into place.

**In Cameroon now, when you talk of political parties, it's the SDF, UNDP, UPC, and CDU. The Social Liberal Congress Party is nowhere and people know not of it. You cannot be nowhere and expect to be at the top.**

The barometer for popularity is a very difficult concept to determine. It is only when the race starts that we will know how popular people are.

It has not been possible for us to enter some of the races that have just taken place, like the 2002 Municipal and Parliamentary elections. Now the Presidential election is coming and, God willing, the Social Liberal Congress will enter the race. I remain confident that if the Social Liberal Congress does its work well on the ground, it will give a good account of itself in the coming races.

**What do you think about the Social Liberal Congress bringing together all the political parties so that they can have a common front?**

That is the strategy towards which the political parties are working. Everybody's wish is that the opposition should be able to produce a single candidate. What are the criteria for selecting such a candidate? We are dealing with a situation in which many factors come into play. People's personal ambitions, hidden intentions, political ideologies; all these obstacles will have to be overcome if the opposition must present a single candidate. As I said earlier, we need a new vision.

**Are you confident of support from French-speaking Cameroonians?**

Although my secondary education was in Saint Joseph's College Sasse, all my university education was in a French-speaking university in Lausanne, Switzerland. I also spent time in France and today my culture is a perfect blend of the Anglophone and the Francophone and I am happy about this.

**Where do you get money to finance this project?**

To tell you the truth, money is secondary in politics. Clear vision is primordial. You can have the world's money, but if you do not have a clear idea of what you want to do with that money it will not serve any purpose. On the contrary, a good product always finds a buyer. The Social Liberal Congress, like most other parties in Cameroon, can maintain its presence on the ground. We have not addressed our minds to money yet. The Party was not founded for monetary reasons.

## *What message do you have for Cameroonians now?*

*All that I can say is that our seeds have remained above ground for too long. We should make them grow. Our destiny is in our hands: Cameroon will be what it will be because Cameroonians shall have made it what it is. I know my countrymen: they are hardworking and they are welcoming. These are great values on which we can base our march forward. I remain confident that when the right time comes, Cameroonians will rise to the new challenge.*

* * *

The recurrent concern of this interview is work. I was happy with the avenue Miss Tambenkongho offered me to drive home the importance of work as the primary strategy for social progress. Any developmental paradigm that is not founded on this strategy cannot provide the necessary safeguards to stagnation or even slump. That is why, in addition to making *work* the opening concept of its Motto, the *Social Liberal Congress* also builds it into the essence of its emblem: a black horse against a gilded background. We know the horse both in mythology and history to be man's friend, not to say man's best friend, in the animal world. In all its generic categories, the horse serves man with selfless dedication. Its life is coterminous with work. But it is also a beautiful thing to behold. Watch the way its magnificent power ripples to the innocent caress of children. The black horse in the *SLC* emblem represents the black race. Gold, for its part, is wealth. The underlying message in the combination is therefore that the black race is worth gold. But then, gold is not something one picks up just like that, effortlessly. It lies deep in the earth's crust and takes quite some digging to reach. You have to *go* for it. Gold-digging is no joke: it calls for work, hard work.

While recognizing the intrinsic endowments of the black race, the *Social Liberal Congress* cautions against sloth and unrewarding occupations. The black race must learn to work like other races. All too often we wait for others to do our work for us. We are forever at the receiving end; and even when we are made to work, we do so in the service of others, never in our own. Our hands, our *minds,* especially, must reach for the gold that we are worth, must work for it. The great nations of this earth admit of no other conditions for their greatness outside work and honest husbandry.

# 6
## The October 2004 Presidential elections

Elections are the marketplace where political parties sell their ideologies. The elected buyers, must it be said, are the people; and franchise, that is to say the ballot paper, their money. Armed with their ballot paper, the voters examine the political ideologies and programmes on offer and buy, that is to say vote for, the one that best appeals to them in terms of its ability to protect their interests. Having voted for such a programme, they then take it home so that their lives thereafter become governed by it. That is why there is no worse crime against democratic practice than to deprive the citizens of their right to vote the political programme of their choice, or to deny them the free enjoyment of such a programme once they have voted it.

Each time voters detect a discrepancy between their voting and its outcome, they manifest their displeasure, at times violently. The 1992 presidential elections produced just such a situation. Violent demonstrations tore through the North West Province at the proclamation of the results and although the rest of the country did not openly express the same reproof, the seething mood was no less indignant. Democracy is a crystal absolute that magnifies the least blot into a scarlet cloak of shame.

The programme that each party markets summarizes its ideals for the society. This programme grows out of a close scrutiny of past and present, and seeks to correct pitfalls while consolidating strengths.

The Motto of the *Social Liberal Congress* rests on a 17-point Manifesto that seeks constant recourse to the will of the citizenry. The preamble to the Manifesto states: *The Social Liberal Congress, the citizen's Party which believes in the cardinal virtues of Work, Justice and Progress, hereby resolves to build a Cameroonian nation dedicated to the citizen.* This set goal then yields the following programme:

1) A decentralized State with semi-autonomous Regions.

2) A semi-presidential system with independent legislative and judiciary powers.

3) An independent electoral commission.

4) Non-participation of traditional rulers in partisan politics.

5) Members of government, of the judiciary, and senior civil servants who declare their assets, liabilities and interest in any undertaking or enterprise.

6) A President of the Republic elected by universal suffrage for a five-year mandate renewable once.

7) Two-round presidential elections and victory by simple majority.

8) A Prime Minister appointed by the President of the Republic on the proposition of the Parliamentary majority and answerable to Parliament.

9) Parliamentarians elected by universal suffrage in single-member constituencies, these constituencies being carved out by population density.

10) A National Assembly with independent powers, that legislates and sanctions government action, and controls the Executive.

11) An independent Judiciary that guarantees legality and the respect of the Constitution.

12) A Constitution that is the supreme law of the land. Drawn up by a constitutional commission, it shall be adopted by referendum.

13) Governors elected by the Regions they administer according to the laws of the Republic.

14) A free-market economy in which private investment shall be encouraged mainly through tax incentives, low customs tariffs, and minimal government intervention.

15) A government that shall protect minority interests and promote the social status of women, children, youths, old people, and the disabled.

16) An educational policy that ensures free primary education and lays stress on science and technology as agents of progress.

17) Transport and communications policies which give priority to roads and telecommunications as means through which to achieve meaningful and lasting development.

On 20 August 2004 the country woke to the news that the SDF Chairman for the Balikumbat Electoral District, Mr John Kohtem, had been beaten to death. This incident provides a befitting illustration of the purpose of manifestos in politics.

The special SDF National Executive Committee, NEC, Resolution of 28 August 2004 on the matter stated:

> *Considering the murder of Mr. John Kohtem on 20 August 2004, following a political meeting with the Governor of the North West Province, at which Mr. Kohtem had death threats from Fon Doh Gah Gwanyin III, MP for Ngoketunjia South Constituency, Mayor of Balikumbat and Member of the Central Committee of the CPDM;*
>
> *Considering that these death threats were a result of the accusations levelled on Fon Doh Gah Gwanyin by Mr. Kohtem, for undertaking parallel registration of voters in Balikumbat, for his tyranny and for his stifling of the democratic process;*
>
> *Considering the protest demonstrations that have been held in Bamenda and elsewhere to demand that justice be done to the murderers of Mr. Kohtem;*
>
> *Considering the condolence visit paid to the family of Mr. Kohtem in Balikumbat on 24 August 2004 by the Leaders of the Coalition for National Reconciliation and Reconstruction;*
>
> *Considering the indignation, solidarity and compassion shown at the national and international levels,*
>
> THE NATIONAL EXECUTIVE COMMITTEE:
>
> *Vehemently condemns this other heinous crime of murder perpetrated on a member of the opposition in Cameroon;*

*Vehemently condemns the culture of impunity nurtured and promoted by the CPDM regime in Cameroon, as manifested by the unpunished assassinations of many Cameroonians, including:*
Hon. Haman Adama in Mayo Rey;
Hon. Martin Esseme in Kumba; and
Mr. John Kohtem in Balikumbat;
*Notes that this murder further highlights the serious problems that bedevil the electoral process in Cameroon, especially the registration of voters where Fons, "chefs de quartiers" and other barons of the CPDM, who are not members of the commissions for the revision of electoral registers, carry out parallel registration in the field.*

\* \* \*

His Royal Highness Fon Doh Gah Gwanyin III is the paramount ruler of Balikumbat. As a traditional ruler, he embodies the collective weal of his people irrespective of their political sympathies. Such an attribute is definitely at variance with partisan politics. As a human being he may want to involve himself in active politics. It is the duty of government to discourage such ambitions given the dangers that they pose to the social cohesion of his fondom. The death of John Kohtem, unfortunately, is just one other pointer to what happens when the leadership of traditional society becomes partisan. All said and done, the death of John Kohtem is to be placed, not at the door of any human being, but at that of the system that makes it possible for a father to discriminate among his children, to the point of rejoicing at the death of one of them. The *Social Liberal Congress* does not condone, much less encourage, such a system. That much is spelled out in point 4 of its Manifesto, which rules out the participation of traditional rulers in partisan politics.

No matter how attractive a party's programme is, such a programme remains ineffective unless it is translated into concrete action. For this to happen, the party must win power. It is only through the exercise of power that a party can put its programme to the test.

The *Social Liberal Congress* came into legal existence on 13 June 2000. By the time the twin parliamentary and municipal elections were organized in June 2002 the Party was just two years old and still quite unknown. It could therefore not enter the race and hope to make a mark. And so it did not. Presidential elections lay just two years ahead. The Party therefore resolved to step up its groundwork mainly through active participation in national events, field activity, and diplomatic tours.

The National Day celebrations of 20 May 2004 provided a good occasion to assess the party's growth rate. On this day the *Social Liberal Congress* marched in the nation's capital, Yaounde; in three of the country's ten provincial capitals: Buea, Douala, Bamenda; in two divisional capitals: Limbe and Kumba; and in one sub-divisional capital: Bali. By all indications, it had come into full-blown existence. It was now ready for the presidential elections.

# 7
## The National Coalition for Reconciliation and Reconstruction (NCRR)

The dying months of 2003 and the early ones of 2004 were employed by the different political parties on the national scene to plot electoral strategies ahead of the presidential elections of October 2004. One such strategy was to pool resources into a common front against the ruling CPDM party.

The electoral code allowed for only a one-round election in which whoever emerged first by whatever percentage was declared winner. In 1992 Paul Biya had been declared winner with 39%. Under such circumstances, and given the tight hold the regime had on the electoral process, no single opposition candidate could launch a successful challenge against the incumbent. As a result, opposition parties thought out a way of circumventing the difficulty: they would create alliances and throw in whatever weight they could muster behind a single candidate.

One such alliance was the *National Coalition for Reconciliation and Reconstruction, NCRR*, which the *Social Liberal Congress* joined on 9 August 2004. It had begun sometime in October 2003 as a bilateral venture between the Social Democratic Front, SDF, of John Fru Ndi, and the Cameroon Democratic Union, CDU, of Adamou Ndam Njoya. At the time of our coming on board, it had grown into the single most important opposition movement that comprised: John Fru Ndi, SDF; Adamou Ndam Njoya, CDU; Yondo Marcel, MLDC; Jean Pahai, PPC; Sanda Oumarou, Issa Tchiroma, Antar Gassagay, all of la Dynamique du Nord; Mukuri Maka, MDP; UPC-Hogbe Nlend; UNDP- Bedzigui; and Sindjoun Pokam of the Civil Society.

Our reasons for joining the NCRR were provided in an elaborate interview we accorded *The Post* newspaper on 3 September 2004, and which we reproduce here below.

**The Post: Your party has just joined the coalition of opposition parties. How did this happen?**

Dr Nyamndi: Yes, the Social Liberal Congress, SLC, formally joined the National Coalition for Reconciliation and Reconstruction on August 9, 2004. It was not an easy decision to take, both for the *Party* and for its leadership. We realized that the country's sympathy was centred on a certain number of parties which were seen to be working in the genuine interest of the country. We thought that if we had to make a useful contribution to the ongoing struggle, the Coalition was where such a contribution could be made.

**Why didn't you join the Presidential Majority?**

Politics has to do with choices and your choice is determined by the interest you pursue at any given moment. The Presidential Majority is pursuing the fight for a better future for Cameroon in its own way. We are not within the logic of mutual exclusion. If the Coalition and the Presidential Majority can each in its own separate way work for the betterment of Cameroon, why not? We are not in an "either or" situation. We are rather interested in ensuring that wherever we are, the interest of Cameroon is uppermost in our considerations.

**In political arrangements like that there is something like give and take. What is it that you negotiated for?**

To be frank with you, we did not join the Coalition with the view to making gains for the Party. We joined the Coalition because we were convinced that the interest of this country could be best preserved, best protected, best taken care of, by the Coalition. If your decision to contribute to the well-being of the country is taken in terms of how the struggle will benefit your party, then your considerations are definitely not genuine. You know we place Cameroon first.

**Before joining the Coalition you had a goal or target. What's this goal or target?**

As I just said, if we have a goal, it is ensuring that the socio-economic situation of our country takes a qualitative leap. Now, how that leap comes about is what all of us, my colleagues and I, are bent on examining. We should not place our individual interest before the common good.

**The Coalition would have designated its candidate before now. Cameroonians would have had time to assess him. It can't just come up with a candidate say a month to the election and expect him to be endorsed.**

Yes, you are right. The question of the single candidate is crucial not only to the survival of the Coalition but indeed to the interest of the country. It is true that Cameroonians are expecting the single candidate a lot, but this depends on who that candidate is; and that's why the Coalition is taking its time to make sure that when it does choose a candidate, that candidate will meet and articulate the aspirations of Cameroonians.

**But it will be coming too late.**

I don't know whether it will be too late, but I think that it will be important that the choice be made carefully rather than rush and make a poor choice. We know that now in Cameroon not just anybody from anywhere can be the president of the country. There are a certain number of criteria which the Coalition have put in place to guide us in the choice of such a candidate. Let me say between the ideal conditions on paper and the real conditions in the field, there is a gap and it is that gap that the Coalition is interested in filling. But I'm sure that given the sincerity with which all the party leaders are tackling the matter of a single candidate, we will choose one which will do Cameroon proud.

**Are you eyeing that position?**

Let me say that the purpose of any politician is the acquisition of power. If I did not have presidential ambitions, I won't be a politician. Every political leader thinks of attaining the highest office of the land one day. That is the driving force behind politics. Now, we are in a democratic situation and we know that democracy has to do with choices made by people, by the largest number; so, who that candidate is does not depend on Nyamndi. It depends on the Coalition, and given their wisdom and foresight, it is my strong belief that when the time comes they will choose the right person.

**But you are a political light weight as compared to the sizes and ages of the other parties. Is eyeing that position not an inordinate ambition?**

Let me make a fundamental correction here. We are dealing with presidential elections, not parliamentary or municipal elections. The president of the country is the person whose profile has to be approved by the country. Popularity as far as I am concerned becomes a secondary consideration. Not every political party leader can be the president of the country. I think we are dealing with paradigms that are different and paradigms that require totally different parameters. If we were talking about parliamentary elections, I could say yes, we are still a young party in the race. And I think Cameroonians are sufficiently clever to be able to see the good person to be that president when he appears.

**What makes you think you can be presidential material?**

If I did not believe that I had the makings of the president of Cameroon, I wouldn't have entered politics in the first place. The president of this country has a profile. Cameroonians know who their president can be and they tell the president when they see him. It continues to be my belief that we will make a right choice. There is a momentum that is gathering towards the discovery of that person. Generally, the papers talk about the rare bird but I think the momentum will end up with the discovery of that rare bird.

**Becoming a president is by election and when we talk of election we talk of numbers. Indeed what is the strength of your party, what is it doing, especially in the face of the prevalent apathy?**

Apathy is relative. I've been talking to a cross section of Cameroonians and my feeling is that they are interested in the elections. Many of them have registered. Let nobody be fooled. My worry is not whether the people are registering. My biggest worry is whether those who have registered will indeed be given their chance. I think that's where the problem is.

**What are you doing about that?**

We have encouraged people to register and they are registering. They see that there is a reason to register and vote. Now, the Social Liberal Congress is not part of the election mechanism. We can only just hope that what the Administration is telling us is genuine. If we go by the reaction on the ground, there is every reason to believe that Cameroonians are waiting for the elections and that they will take part in their large numbers. Only the Administration can answer that question.

**You say you have been talking to people and encouraging them to vote. I don't remember or know of any rally you have held to convince the people.**

Public rallies have their own role to play but groundwork is even more important when you talk to people on a man-to-man basis. We need to go meet the people where they are. It is not only in rallies that you can sensitize the electorate. Initiatives outside the traditional forms of sensitization are important. Party militants and party cadres are in the field practically all over the country encouraging Cameroonians to register. Of course, you don't expect them to run to you each time and say I've told this person to register and he has registered. They know that if the electorate does not respond actively and with conviction, the election will not go the way we expect. But I think we've done a good job making Cameroonians become aware of what lies ahead of them. And they have given us all the assurances that they know the importance of the upcoming election and they will play their part as citizens.

**Going in for the election, do you think NEO will deliver the goods?**

NEO to me is just one of those mechanisms put in place to create the impression that democracy is taken seriously in Cameroon. Its mission has not been given to it. What Cameroon needs at the present state of democratic evolution is not an observatory. Cameroon needs an election-organizing mechanism. A mechanism that makes the playing field level for everybody. NEO is like a hunter without a gun: he cannot shoot, much less kill. It should be given independence and the power to organize elections and control them from the beginning to the end.

**You are an Anglophone and you know that there is an Anglophone problem which puts the unity of the Cameroons at stake. How do you assess this vis-à-vis the election, the party, and the Coalition?**

For those who know me, being an Anglophone is just as important a part of my life as being a Francophone, but my origin commands that I take special interest in the conditions of Anglophones in Cameroon. That is why each time I have had the occasion, I have made it clear that the Anglophone problem is a serious one and one that needs to be addressed with the kind of seriousness that it requires. Now, this having been said, Anglophones are not an island. Cameroon is also made up of Francophones. They also have their problems. Now, at the same time as we address the Anglophone problem, we will also need to address the Francophone problem too. I do not believe in the idea of disintegration because I know that deep down, Anglophones are patriots. They love their country. That is why they chose to reunite with Francophones in the first place. If they are complaining, it is simply because their own aspirations have not properly been taken into account. I have a strong conviction that the minute the aspirations of Anglophones are taken into account, the Anglophone problem will go away by itself.

**Basically when you say there is an Anglophone problem as much as there is a Francophone problem, you are dismissing the fact that Anglophones have a problem. A problem of marginalization.**

No. That's why I have placed the two components of this country side by side. I did it knowingly. The tendency is for people to oppose the Anglophone to the Beti man or the Bamileke man. No. The opposite of an Anglophone is not a Beti man or a Douala man. The opposite of an Anglophone is a Francophone. We have a special problem in Cameroon which is one of neglect. That neglect will be taken care of once things are done properly at the national level. But let me also point out that neglect in Cameroon is not specific to the Anglophones; which does not mean, though, that the Anglophone neglect is not important. But we should not be blinded to the other problems that may – and do – exist in Francophone Cameroon.

**How do you see the SCNC which has been articulating this Anglophone problem?**

The people who keep the SCNC alive are Cameroonians. They are human beings. They are intelligent and courageous people. The movement has a raison d'être. The SCNC should be listened to. They have a story to tell. I'm not sure that the system in place now has taken the right approach. You don't solve a problem by looking away. Not listening to people will not stop them from complaining and I think the SCNC is doing a good job by keeping the Anglophone problem alive.

**Some Southern Cameroonians abroad have formed the Ambazonia Liberation Party to articulate the problem. How do you see it?**

A serious problem such as the Anglophone problem must be tackled from all the angles possible to enhance the Anglophone condition in Cameroon. If the purpose of the party is to solve the problem, then it is a useful addition to the political landscape of Cameroon.

**What message do you have for the Coalition, the electorate and for those who have not yet registered?**

The message is the same for everybody. The SCNC is a political movement in Cameroon and Cameroon is the boat in which all Cameroonians are. If that boat sinks, all of us will sink, including the Head of State. My plea is that all Cameroonians, irrespective of the political party to which they belong, should place the common good of this country before their individual interests. People who have not registered because they think there is nothing to vote for should register because Cameroon has a miracle in store for them. When the new dawn breaks, those who did not believe in it will say to themselves: if I had known! It is yet time to be part of the game!

This interview was granted against the background of gathering uncertainty and intensifying apprehension. The presidential elections were just two months away but no official statement had as yet been made about them. Given the one-man-band nature of government, in which the fate of an entire nation depended on the whims and caprices of one man, the President of the Republic, only he could make such a statement, pending which all the rest of us could do was speculate and project.

* * *

Joining the Coalition brought me into direct contact with the psychology of Cameroonian politics. I came to discover that, contrary to all appearances, political affiliations were still very strongly ethnic in their drive. People still joined political parties or voted according to tribal allegiances. For example, when it came to choosing a unique candidate for the NCRR, each main cultural group staked a claim to the ticket. The Grand North maintained that since their region was the most densely populated in the country, it would be normal that such a candidate issue from there. They argued further that if the population of the Grand North did not identify with the candidate, culturally, that is, they would not vote for him. It did not matter to them that Ahmadou Ahidjo had ruled the country for 21 years, and that the failed coup attempt of 1984 made a return of power to the North a most unlikely happening given the fear of reprisal nursed by the ruling Beti clan. The Grand South for its part stated categorically that since power was in their hands, only another candidate from the Beti clan could defeat Paul Biya. It did not matter to them either that Paul Biya had ruled the country for 22 years and that it would be awkward, to say the least, to expect the rest of the country to underwrite the confiscation of power by one clan.

Since reunification in 1961 the country had been in the hands of successive francophone presidents; first Ahmadou Ahidjo until 1982, then Paul Biya ever since then. At no time in the course of the Coalition search for a unique candidate did any Francophone political leader suggest, even remotely, that an Anglophone candidate could be chosen. On the contrary, there seemed to be a tacit and ardent contract that barred the way firmly to any such possibility. No-one seemed ready to pay any heed to the Anglophone cry for its turn at the helm of state. And yet it seemed clear that after 43 years of unbroken Francophone rule, the time had come to give Anglophones a chance. Try as he might, the valiant Fru Ndi could not get this point of view across to the other Francophone leaders of the Coalition. They were all agreed that Biya had to go, but they were all equally agreed that he had to be replaced by yet another Francophone, and each one of them saw himself in that Francophone!

Somehow, though, what the leaders of the Coalition seemed to resent was not so much the principle of Anglophone leadership as the man who incarnated that leadership at the time: John Fru Ndi.

When the *Social Liberal Congress* joined the Coalition we immediately made it clear that we were not in the race for the Coalition ticket and that we would wholeheartedly support whoever emerged as the flag-bearer. The element of rivalry and its corollary of suspicion and mistrust having thus been cleared, the other leaders took us into their confidence and opened up substantially. From our interactions with them we gathered that in general, they begrudged the SDF leader his unremitting monolingualism; in fact some of them judged his attitude to the French language condescending.

Of all the Coalition leaders, Fru Ndi was the only one who needed the aid of an interpreter to understand his Francophone peers, but who in return spoke in English in the conviction that that language was either intelligible to all or had to be. His Francophone peers bemoaned the fact that in his fourteen years of active politics ever since the heydays of the 90s, he had not made any conscious effort to bridge the language gap between himself and the majority Francophone population. As a result they all came to the conclusion that he did not deem Francophones and their language worthy of his trouble. They also found him somewhat overbearing, even dictatorial.

To buttress the fact that their problem was with the man Fru Ndi and not the Anglophone culture as such, the Francophone leaders in the Coalition pointed to the 1992 presidential elections in which Francophones and Anglophones voted massively for Fru Ndi. He would have been president but for other extra-democratic considerations, foremost among which was precisely his unfamiliarity with French language and culture! The intervening years between 1992 and 2004 had provided them with enough observation time to pick holes in Fru Ndi's character and political attitude.

*The National Coalition for Reconciliation and Reconstruction* brought us into contact with a rich array of political figures, many of whom had made a lasting impression on the political consciousness of the people. Adamou Ndam Njoya, Issa Tchiroma, Jean Pahai, Sanda Oumarou, Antar Gassagay, Sindjoun Pokam, Mokouri Maka, Yondo Marcel, Celestin Bedzigui, Tazoacha Asonganyi, these were all household names in Cameroonian politics. They had, each in their own way, advanced the cause of democracy in an otherwise highly resistant terrain.

Interacting with people of different socio-cultural and even ideological provenances is one of the most rewarding dividends in politics. The exhilarating encounter of opinions and visions, the ballet of ambitions and hopes, all combine to give the moments of political communion a flavour all their own.

Ever since the introduction of multiparty politics in Cameroon, one man has stood out, stood out so very distinctly that he has become one with the history of democratic struggle in Cameroon. That man is John Fru Ndi. Since he raised his clenched right fist in Bamenda on 26 May 1990 and, amid bloodshed, broke the spell of monolithism, the collective political unconscious has hailed him, glorified him, even deified him. And with reason. His intrepid nationalism freed the minds of Cameroonians from long years of debilitating tyranny and made it possible for people to accede to freedom of expression and association.

Cameroon owes the essence of its democratic experience to John Fru Ndi; and so do many people their unhoped-for places in the pages of Cameroonian history. He has made Prime Ministers without himself ever having been one. He has moved the balance of power around and brought new political forces to bear in a landscape that had been heretofore humdrum in its predictability. He stands apart, tall over everyone else in his passionate quest for the well-being of a people in whom his own very existence is lost.

We were both humbled and thankful to the NCRR for making us share in this man's unique vision for his country. Whether or not Fru Ndi ever becomes president of Cameroon is immaterial. He is already President, because he has been so anointed by the people. And a people's unction is eternal.

On 24 August 2004 Christian Cardinal Tumi, Archbishop of Douala, granted audience to an NCRR delegation made up of Yondo Marcel, Moukouri Maka, Issa Tchiroma, Sanda Oumarou, Jean Pahai, and myself. We had come to thank the man of God for his crusade for justice and peace, and to ask for his continued prayers for the country. He accepted to pray for Cameroon, and gave us two criteria to guide us in the choice of a candidate for the presidential elections: such a person should be bilingual and god-fearing. These to me were the two most salient qualities that no-one honestly interested in the future of Cameroon could afford to overlook. Interestingly enough, the Coalition had not thought it necessary to underscore bilingualism as a fundamental criterion for eligibility. And yet Cameroon's image as a member of the Commonwealth and of the Francophonie, it seemed to us, stood to gain from such a profile. Forty-three years into the experience of national integration or national coexistence as one chose, was there any sense in perpetrating the embarrassment – not to say the provocative arrogance – of presidential monolingualism in a constitutionally and socially bi-cultural state?

Choosing a unique candidate for the Coalition was a grave duty. Everyone was aware of that. The first thing I impressed on my colleagues immediately upon my admission into the Coalition was that power in Cameroon was not a ping-pong game between North and South. I reminded them that Cameroon was a triangle, and that as we all knew, a triangle had three sides. Following this geometric design, it stood to reason that after the North and the South, the baton of power had to be handed over to the West, and more specifically to Anglophone Cameroon. This reasoning did not find favour with most of the leaders, who, outside Fru Ndi and myself, were of Francophone extraction. But I knew that I was echoing public opinion and historical justice.

On Saturday 11 September 2004 I was travelling to Bamenda to attend the extraordinary convention of the SDF to which I had been expressly invited by Ni John Fru Ndi. Somewhere into Bangante I received a phone call from my brother Samuel Fohtung informing me that Biya had just issued a decree inviting the electorate to the polls on 11 October 2004. The document was purportedly signed in Yaounde, at a time when the signatory himself was still away in Europe, possibly in Paris, where he had been holed up for close to one month. He did not return to the country until Sunday 12 September, in the full view of a stunned nation, and totally at home with the paradox of his ubiquity.

The Coalition settled down to the business of choosing a candidate on Monday 13 September. The SLC had held an extraordinary convention the previous day and resolved that I be its candidate for the Coalition ticket. This was a sudden development which the Coalition had not expected since all along I had maintained that I was not interested in the ticket, a stance which certainly influenced the game plans of the other leaders.

I reached Yaounde on Monday 13 September at 5 pm, just in time to tender my candidature before the electoral college went into a closed-door session. I was the fifth in line, the other four candidates being Ni John Fru Ndi (SDF), Adamou Ndam Njoya (CDU), Sanda Oumarou (ARN), and Yondo Marcel (MLDC).

The electoral college was chaired by Issa Tchiroma and comprised Mokouri Maka (MDP), Jean Pahai (PRR), Antar Gassagay, Celestin Bedzigui, Henri Hogbe Nlend, Sindjoun Pokam, Henri Bebe Njoh, and Tazoacha Asonganyi.

It is no accident that only Mokouri Maka and Jean Pahai have been mentioned together with the political parties they headed. This is because they were bona fide leaders of political parties just like the other five members of the Coalition who had declared their candidature for the ticket. As for the rest, it was difficult to ascertain in what capacity they sat on the electoral college and what criteria qualified them for such a portentous mission. The absence of agreed conditions for eligibility as electors was perhaps the most devastating weakness of the entire Coalition venture. In throwing the doors of the electoral college open to just anybody who cared to join it, the Coalition deprived itself of the force of objectivity and made room for betrayal and sabotage. One came to see more and more that most of the electors were there for anything but the good of the Coalition. Rather than apply themselves to the delicate job of choosing a good candidate for the looming test, some of the electors donned their caps of infiltrators and openly worked to frustrate the success of the exercise. Candidates were insulted, derided, maligned and ridiculed by persons whose sole business in the Coalition was to boost their personal ambitions and guarantee the failure of the venture.

The electoral college comprised only one Anglophone, SDF Secretary General Tazoacha Asonganyi. It was clear from this configuration that when the time came for the cultural tug-of-war, he would be swept off his feet and easily across the line of assimilation; for the whole exercise went on against a thinly-veiled background of prejudices and stereotypes, the genuine conviction of SDF members of the college notwithstanding.

The battle for a unique candidate lasted until Tuesday 14 September at midnight. The candidates met at 4 pm on that same Tuesday in Ndam Njoya's office to work out a compromise. Each one of us spoke passionately about the need for sacrifice and patriotism, but at the end none of us budged from his claim to the ticket. By 7pm we had still not broken the stalemate, so the matter was sent back to the electoral college for arbitration. As for us the candidates, we took a brief break and returned at 8pm to continue the increasingly hopeless search for a consensus. We did not reach one. All hopes were now on the electoral college.

As one of the strategies to facilitate the choice of a candidate, the Coalition had established the following criteria against which each candidate would be measured for suitability:

Good communication skills
Established international aura
Solvency
Love of country
Physical and moral health
Honesty, integrity, composure
Aptitude for dialogue, debate and team work.
Personal achievement
Courage and fighting spirit
Personality
Popularity in and outside the country

Commitment to change
Management skills
Commitment to democracy
Age (at least 50)

The candidates were to be scored along these criteria and at the end the one with the highest score would be automatically declared the NCRR candidate.

These criteria had a few serious shortcomings. First of all, they did not take into account the geo-politics of the country as they left one with the impression that the President of Cameroon at this particular point in time, that is to say after Ahidjo and Biya, could come from just any part of the country. Such a view did not take due account of the smouldering animosities occasioned by the failed coup attempt of April 1984 and the subsequent reprisals, and of the legitimate ambitions of the other parts of the country still waiting for their own turn at the helm of state. Any search for a candidate for the presidency of this country that turned a blind eye to the important issue of geo-politics and historical justice could not bear fruit.

Secondly, the criteria were silent on the important question of bilingualism. They made tenuous reference to communication skills but failed to state clearly what those skills entailed. Did they mean by communication skills the ability to speak one of the two official languages well? Or the ability to speak to Cameroonians in both official languages? The nuance was important, especially given the repeated battering that the image of Cameroon had suffered on the international scene on account of the lopsided manner in which that image was projected. The impression was always given that Cameroon was a monocultural (Francophone) country even if the historical and cultural records were there to prove the contrary. The result was that official language policies paid only very little attention to linguistic balance. One would have expected the criteria to address this shortcoming resolutely by making it clear that the would-be candidate had to be able to communicate with his people in both official languages. That this was not done proved how unwilling the Coalition was to address the fundamental issues plaguing the unity of the country.

Shortly before midnight the Chairman of the electoral college came to us with the results of the elections. But before he announced them he said my candidature had not been examined because the college had considered that I was still too new in the Coalition to be eligible for its ticket. Startling revelation. A new clause had just been tailored to suit my dossier. I had not been judged too new when it had come to marching down the streets of Yaounde every Tuesday with the other leaders of the Coalition, at great risk to our lives, to demand the computerization of electoral registers; and to making other significant contributions to the cause, including that of helping to design the selection criteria. Even more revealingly, at the same time as I was being disqualified on those spurious grounds, negotiations were going on with people who were not even members of the Coalition. That shabby treatment made it clear to me from that instant on that I was in the wrong place.

I do not know why, but this incident told me in vivid terms just how ill-prepared the country was for the democratic game. The nonchalant readiness with which my candidature was discarded underscored the fact that the search for a suitable candidate was really not the primary concern of the electoral college. When you start looking for reasons to discard candidatures even before you have found a good one, then what you are doing quite simply is looking for reasons to kill your own cause. Having thus laid my candidature to a seething rest, Issa Tchiroma now declared his results which placed Adamou Ndam Njoya first with a score of fifteen on fifteen, followed by Sanda Oumarou with a score of thirteen on fifteen, John Fru Ndi with a score of eleven on fifteen, and Marcel Yondo who scored ten on fifteen.

The classroom touch to the melodrama was a comely reminder of the ultimate emptiness of all political play. Democratic principles, governed as we know by the law of numbers, was expelled from this new scheme of things, and so was historical justice. For this exercise to have any hopes of succeeding, the leader of the most popular party in the Coalition, John Fru Ndi, should have been made the principal actor in the choice of the single candidate. He was instead reduced – or did he reduce himself? - to the role of contender, thereby surrendering his political might to individuals, some of them real political gangsters, who wasted no time to ruin it for him, thoroughly. As an interesting indication of the kind of porous remnant the Coalition had become at this stage, the minute my dossier was rejected by the electoral college, I received a phone-call from outside informing me of the happening; that is to say the election was actually being conducted in the marketplace, with the Coalition's deadliest rivals controlling the turn of events. Shortly after the collapse of the Coalition, Antar Gassagay returned to his home-base and invited his militants to vote for the CPDM candidate! All along, he'd been one of the principle members of the electoral college and by and large the most 'committed' and 'enthusiastic' member of the Coalition whose altruism had endeared him to many, including myself.

In the absence of Fru Ndi's blessing, I failed to see how the chosen candidate could make any headway. Fru Ndi may never be king; he is the anointed king-maker!

Sanda Oumarou immediately endorsed the results. Marcel Yondo said he would do so only after he had taken cognizance of the package deal that had been agreed. Fru Ndi expressed his (understandable) sense of affront, disclaimed the results, and stormed out followed by Mbah Ndam who had replaced Atekwana as his interpreter that day. As Fru Ndi left, a tremor of failure overwhelmed me. I saw months of effort brought to naught. But that was not my most immediate worry. The journalists waiting outside to take the news to the country. What were we going to tell them? And Cameroonians. What were we going to say we had done with their dreams? I felt horrible. I carried my mind back to the moments we had spent together as a team: Bamenda where we'd thrilled the boiling crowd with our promise to fight even to the last man; Balikumbat where we had demonstrated an extraordinary sense of union in the face of a bloody adversity; Yaounde; Douala.

My sadness was redeemed somehow by the realization of the tremendous odds that the Coalition faced. We knew all along that not everybody who proclaimed their commitment to the cause believed in it. We knew that greed and treachery would be unleashed on the venture as the moment of choice drew nearer.

I followed shortly after Fru Ndi's exit in a less spectacular manner, but in a no less spectacular show of discontent. Fru Ndi and I were the lone Anglophone candidates in the race. As I drove back home that night I kept wondering why there was always such a persistent design to block the way of Anglophones to leadership in Cameroon. That spell had to be broken, somehow!

Quite a lot has been said about Fru Ndi's reaction to the choice of the Coalition candidate. Some people have felt that he allowed his emotions to overshadow his reason; some that he was greedy; yet others that he lacked sportsmanship. Some people even think that his reaction was unpatriotic since he betrayed the pact signed by the Coalition leaders to keep the team together come what may.

All these accusations are not without relevance, but they do not paint the full picture of the saga.

Like all proud and charismatic men, Fru Ndi is an emotional person. His pride is founded on a high sense of achievement and indispensability, and he does not see how or why he should watch events from the sidelines. He belongs in the epicentre of all political action! Yes, there was a strong emotional edge to the stormy walk-out, but when a proud man is cut to the quick, the reaction, more often than not, is likely to be emotional. He could be taken to task for having failed to give dialogue a chance at such a fragile moment in the life of the Coalition.

Fru Ndi's reaction may have struck the ordinary mind as greedy, especially after he had subjected himself to the vote. But then one has to understand that intuition is also a reliable guide. And Fru Ndi is an intuitive man. He felt and knew that without the Coalition ticket in his firm grip, the population he represented would lose interest in the venture; and that under the circumstances, that would be the end of the Coalition hopes for victory in the elections.

Sportsmanship in a country of sportsmen is revealing of our personal psychologies. Cameroonians on the whole take defeat very badly. I've known cases of persons who have dropped dead in front of their TV screens because the final whistle has carried victory away from home. The champion in all of us, coupled with the proud side of us, just cannot accommodate defeat, especially in the hands of lesser forces. The Cameroonian is proud in a unique way. This pride has made him achieve some really great things; but it has also cost him some finer rewards.

Fru Ndi is the last person anyone will term unpatriotic. In fact he is patriotism incarnate and this is what has kept him going. My own conviction is that Fru Ndi did not lose the Coalition ticket on the day the electoral college chose someone else. He lost that ticket the day he allowed himself to contest for it with other candidates. In politics you don't put your strength on the scale. If you know you are invincible, remain invincible. Don't challenge anyone, no matter how insignificant, to a fight. The SDF should have made it clear from the word go that any parties joining it in a coalition were doing so on the firm understanding that the SDF would remain the hub of such a coalition and that the choice of a presidential candidate would be its (the SDF's) sole business. Any party joining them at that time would have known that Fru Ndi would be the presidential candidate of their coalition. This was not done and everybody came with the secret intention of riding to power on the back of SDF popularity. At the end of the day, the SDF only have themselves to blame for their debacle. In politics, there is no room for mistakes of analysis. De telles erreurs se paient cash!

On Thursday 16 September 2004 the SLC pulled out of the Coalition and announced that it was entering the presidential race with its National President as its candidate. The press release that broke the news also implored the guidance of the Almighty on its candidate, on the Party, and on the entire Cameroonian nation. This was in the normal order of things, for everything issues from God and returns to Him.

Forty-six candidates registered for the presidential race. On Monday 20 September 2004 Cardinal Tumi granted me audience at his home in the Douala Archdiocese. We spent some thirty minutes discussing current political issues and especially the Coalition stalemate caused by the Fru Ndi-Ndam Njoya standoff. The Cardinal was deeply saddened at the turn of things and wished the two leaders had stepped aside in favour of a neutral candidate still drawn from within the ranks of the Coalition. To him, the two political leaders were more of neutralizing forces against each other than enabling drives to the Coalition cause.

I stepped out of the Cardinal's office at 4.30 pm. At 5pm the national radio announced that sixteen candidates had been retained for the presidential race. I was one of them. My mind went back to the audience with the Cardinal.

There is very little one can say about Cardinal Tumi because the man thinks so little of himself that it would be indecent to say more than he himself would. But during the audience I reminded him of the Convocation discourse he delivered to the third batch of graduating students at the University of Buea on 21 December 1998, and which I take delight in reproducing here as a fitting beacon to these reflections.

But before I do so, and especially since I am talking about the University of Buea, let me talk about one person under whose stewardship as Vice Chancellor I have spent the last eleven years of my life. Greatness is not only in the great things we do but in the little acts we accomplish in the service of great causes. In 1995 Lady Dorothy Limunga Njeuma procured me a French Cooperation grant for a three-month stay at the Université Stendhal, Grenoble III, for a refresher course in the teaching of French as a foreign language. Immediately upon my return she had me appointed Assessor for A' Level French at the Cameroon GCE Board. In September 2003 I enjoyed a further preferment, this time as Director of Administrative Affairs of the University of Buea. This is not an isolated testimony. Dr. Mrs Dorothy Limunga Njeuma has been in the limelight as academic, politician, administrator and benefactor since 1975 when the late President Ahmadou Ahidjo appointed her Vice Minister of Education. And it is as it should be, for probity does not belong in the dark.

The 1998 Convocation discourse at the University of Buea was on Truth. On that day 21 December I sat one row away from the speaker, my eyes all the time on his white cassock. It was spotless, like the object of his meditation, and rippled every now and again to his gentle emphasis.

*The Honourable Minister of Higher Education*
*and Chancellor of Cameroon State Universities,*
*The Pro-Chancellor,*
*The Vice Chancellor,*
*Distinguished Guests,*
*The Staff and Students,*
*Ladies and Gentlemen,*

*I am grateful to the Vice-Chancellor for inviting me to talk to the third batch of the graduating students of this University which in so short a time is become so well-known. On this solemn occasion, I have chosen to meditate with you on "The Truth," the object of all knowledge. In every scientific inquiry, the one who seeks, looks for the truth, embedded in the nature of things.*

The true scientist may fight against all his passions but treasures one, his passion for the truth. He may master all his passions but one remains his master, his passion for the truth. He knows that to be slave to the truth is to be a free man.

But truth! What is it? Truth is ontological or logical. It is ontological when it concerns the study of the being of things. The stone is. The plant and the animal are. Man and God are. Ontology or the study of being, as such wants to know what we mean when we say a thing is. And since every thing that is, is first in the mind of its creator, ontological truth is therefore defined as the conformity of objective reality with its divine ideal, with its corresponding idea in the mind of the creator.

Related to ontological truth are the truths of the experimental sciences, or scientific principles and laws. All your life as a schoolchild and student has been spent in the search and in the accumulation of these principles and laws which, when obtained by methodical procedure and built into a coherent system, make up scientific knowledge. And this knowledge is never enough. The more you know, the more you want to know. In the academic field when the desire to know ceases, scientific progress ceases.

Dear students, I advise you never to stop studying. Keep on reading and writing. Avoid every habit that weakens the body and the intellect, your memory and the power of the will. Avoid alcohol. Every drop of it, frequently taken, weakens your body and consequently your intellect. Pure water does you no harm. If your body is healthy, your mind and will, will also be healthy. Eat well and just enough. Too much food makes one sleepy and weak, and lazy, and intellectually much less active.

Watch out for causes of error in your search for the truth. The first of these causes could be vanity, by which we have too much confidence in our own ability. Always be ready to accept correction. Only God knows every thing.

The more you know that you do not know, the more you want to know, and the more you progress intellectually. And the more you are aware of your ignorance in many scientific fields, the more intellectually humble you become. And this leads you to humility as a moral virtue.

One of the causes of error could be personal interest by which we accept only assertions which please us. In the search for truth, the *intellectually honest man accepts, not only what pleases but also what displeases him, as long as it is true.*

*Error in reasoning could be caused by laziness, which prevents us from making the necessary effort to look for the truth. There is no easy way to scientific knowledge. Do not accept without control prejudices of day-to-day life, the authority of false scientists, and equivocal language. And never make any categorical affirmation when in doubt. The one who looks for the truth may only act in methodical doubt, that doubt which helps to look for the true and the scientific.*

*How to fight against error in the search for scientific truth! Practise intellectual hygiene, by respecting the laws and rules of correct reasoning, by the control of the imagination and by the development of the memory. Above all, you fight against error by loving the truth.*

*Love for the truth inclines us to judge with perfect impartiality, to proceed with patience, caution and perseverance in the search for the truth.*

*And our dignity as human beings obliges us to seek the truth and especially religious truth. Intellectual honesty leads the scientist to the truth that there must be a supreme intelligence responsible for order in the world, for the perfect organization of the world, for order in every thing that is, moves and grows. Anyone who does not accept this fundamental truth, will find his search for the truth and for the ultimate truth, an impossibility.*

*The scientist creates no scientific law or principle. He discovers the laws governing the visible world as put in it by its creator. One of the proofs of the existence of God, is the intelligent organization of the world. If there were no God, a Supreme intelligent being, man would have to invent one to explain his existence and that of the world and its perfect organization.*

*Once we have known the truth, we are morally bound to adhere to it and to direct our whole life in accordance with its demands.*

*Adhering to the truth is adhering to God. He is the source of all truths. He is truth itself. To deny the existence of God is to deny the existence of any truth. That is why Faith in God and the knowledge of Him help us to know the truth. And reason helps us to understand our faith in God. Any education that negates any of its three objects, knowledge of the material world, of man, and of God, is not whole. If* one has not had some basic general education in theology, one may be a great scientist, but there will be something fundamentally lacking in one's overall intellectual formation. That is why in universities of the Middle Ages and in serious Anglo-Saxon universities, there is always at least a department for religious studies.

Dear students, I have been trying to explain ontological truth. There is also logical truth which is the conformity between the idea man has of a thing and the thing as it exists outside the mind. It is the agreement between what you say and what you think. If there is no conformity between the idea and its expression in words, a lie is told.

One must be true in deeds and in words. That is why truth condemns duplicity, dissimulation and hypocrisy. Not to speak the truth to your neighbour or about him is to be unjust to him. In situations that require witness to the truth, we must profess it without equivocation.

Dear students, in life, beware of false witness and perjury. These offences against the truth in our society, contribute to the "condemnation of the innocent, to the exoneration of the guilty or to increased punishment of the accused. They gravely compromise the exercise of justice and the fairness of judicial decision."

Many who are in prison are innocent, and many criminals are moving around. Never be knowingly responsible for the condemnation of the innocent.

Other offences against truth are rash judgment, that is to say, assuming as true without sufficient foundation the moral fault of a neighbour; detraction, which is, disclosing another's fault without an objectively valid reason, to a person who did not know it; calumny or harming the reputation of another and thus giving occasion for false judgment concerning him by remarks contrary to the truth. Even the greatest of criminals has a right to his human dignity and reputation.

We should however avoid flattery. It confirms your neighbour in his malicious acts and perverse conduct. Have the courage to correct each other but in private.

Lying, which consists in speaking falsehood with the intention of deceiving the one to whom you are speaking, is the most direct offense against the truth. Never lie. A lie is never justifiable.

The purpose of speech is to communicate known truth. To lie is therefore a profanation of speech, the most sacred instrument of social *communication, sacred because created directly by God himself. Speech is God-made.*

Dear students, know that every offense against the truth entails the grave duty of making reparation publicly or secretly. That is to say, if you have committed the offense of rash judgment, of detraction, of calumny, or of lying against anybody, you are bound in justice to do everything possible to restore the person's good name and reputation.

When this is done, you experience a certain inner joy, a joy that is brought about by every good deed. It is beautiful and joyful and worthy of praise to speak the truth. On the contrary, an evil act or lie is the cause of sadness and sickness and disorder in us and in our society.

Truth is that virtue that necessarily carries with it the joy and the splendour of spiritual beauty. "Truth is beautiful in itself." You may be naturally and physically beautiful, but if you are a liar, you become ugly, and your beauty, which should be an image of the spiritual beauty of its creator, becomes disgusting and repulsive.

Moral beauty is excellent. And the truth helps you to have it. To tell a lie is to become an apostle of the father of lies, the Devil.

Love scientific truth. Meditate it when it has been discovered. But love moral truth above all. It makes you beautiful. It gives joy. You may be the best scientist the world has known, but if you have no morals, you are a danger to yourself and to society.

Dear students, you are the light of tomorrow, the light of this nation. You should begin to shine now, by waging war against lying in our society. Do that by words and obviously by a life governed by truth. Know that to embezzle what belongs to the national community is to lie. To falsify a document is to lie. To make people think you are what you are not is to lie. A false certificate or Degree is a practical lie. And you correct that by tearing the certificate!

Where school age is not the same as real age, there is a lie, and the truth is absent. Where some young man or woman is employed, not on the basis of merit but because he or she is the son or daughter of some politician or minister, or top civil servant, there is injustice; and where there is injustice, truth is absent and a lie is necessarily present; and society is deceived.

You came here to look for the truth. You have found it, not all of it, but enough of it to help you begin to search for more of it in life.

*Make sure you continue the search for the truth until you reach the supreme truth which alone satisfies man's intellectual curiosity. Your intellect will never be at rest until it rests in the ultimate truth.*

*Dear students, in your dealings with men and women in society, avoid all detraction and calumny. If you have no good word for a person, silence is best. Be men and women of principles; and never do a thing because others are doing it. Do it because you are convinced it is the right thing to do. Even if you are the only one to do what is right, have the courage to do it even at the cost of your life. You might have been created to be the prophet of your time.*

*Respect the reputation of those with whom you are and work. Do not think you can build yours on the ruins of theirs. That does not work. In trying to destroy the good name of others you destroy your own. A good reputation is built on hard work and merit. It is built on the true and the meritorious.*

*I wish you have one disease, a disease of which I strongly desire you may never be cured. To be cured of it is to be cursed. The disease of which I strongly wish you may never be cured is passion for the truth. May you die because of it!*

*Show yourself true in deeds and truthful in words. And never be ashamed to stand firmly for the truth, wherever you may be.*

*Lying is destructive of man and society. It undermines trust among men and women and friends. And tears apart the whole fabric of social relationship.*

*Truth alone frees and saves. Let it be your stronghold all through life and you will rarely go astray.*

*Christian Cardinal TUMI*
*Archevêque de DOUALA*

I have elected to ride on the moral crest of this discourse because it enfolds the ultimate reward of all human pursuit: happiness. All action is vain unless it puts a smile on the face of human existence. And so if there is anything we can ask of life, it is that it make us the worthy instruments of human happiness.

Christian Cardinal Tumi is one man who has generated more than his own fair share of controversy. Those who love him do so to the point of adoration. Those who hate him want him dead. And it is just as well, for his calling is no sinecure. These clashing views of the same man become reconciled once you come in contact with the person. The man has an overwhelming personality sustained by two passions: his love for man and his faith in truth. He is a good soldier in the service of these two causes, indomitable, except by justice; intrepid, especially before wrong. He is ever ready to excoriate evil, ever poised to give chase to the devil.

This discourse was the last thing I read before I entered the presidential race of October 2004. It was also the main supply of inspiration throughout my campaign. My different addresses to the Cameroonian nation, reproduced herebelow, were anchored in the soil of daily reality and sustained by a collective vision that shone through the debilitating pessimism of the times.

## Opening address

*My dear countrymen,*

*It is with exceeding joy that I share this solemn moment with you. I thank the Almighty God for having ordained it.*

*The President is the single most important person in the collective destiny of any people. That is why utmost care must be taken in electing him. We prosper or perish in the hands of our President.*

*As you go to the polls on 11 October 2004, let nothing but your fatherland be your guide. Think of the children of this country; all of them. Their destiny is in your vote.*

*But before anything else, let me take this opportunity to pay sincere homage to the outgoing President, Mr. Paul Biya. He governed our country for 22 years and leaves behind a legacy that only history will assess. The time has come for him to say goodbye and enjoy a well-deserved rest.*

*As for us, fellow countrymen, we must now take stock and see whether we want to maintain the old ways or break with the past and design a new course that will lead us into a future of justice, love and harmony; one that will reassert our presence on the international scene. I think the choice is self-evident. We must reinvent our society and become ourselves full actors in the exciting experience of nation building.*

God bless you.

In opening and closing this inaugural speech with God I was only respecting the Biblical teaching that in everything we should give thanks to God, and that he labours in vain who does not labour in the Lord. The centrality of the divine in all human effort requires no new emphasis. Often we think our achievements come from our human strength only, and that God is there to be sought, if at all, only in times of adversity. In this connection, the American swearing-in tradition serves as a good example of what powers humility can confer on man's enterprise. The ceremony always ends with the new President saying: "So help me God." In seeking God's help the President of the United States of America, arguably the strongest man on earth in our day, is acknowledging his human weakness and God's omnipotence. Once things and persons are put in their right perspective this way, the march forward becomes logical, predictable: the divine light clears our human steps in our journey through life and both our individual entreaties and commonweal achieve fulfilment at little cost.

The speech also expounds the belief that "the President is the single most important person in the collective destiny of any people." This is all the more so in a country like ours where the Head of State wields inordinate powers. Because practically all the nation's powers are concentrated in the single hands of the President, he becomes a potentate, whether he likes it or not. The absence of checks and balances which an independent judiciary and an equally independent and assertive legislature would provide transforms the President into something of a deity with little or no hold on the reality, often harsh, of his people, and no account whatsoever to render to any mortal. In a situation like this, the President's intrinsic endowments become crucial as they alone can guarantee a human touch to his reign. In a country like Cameroon where the population is numbed and awed by the towering might of the President, a good President becomes a gift from God and one for which the people must pray and pray fervently. That is why the next important thing the speech says is that we prosper or perish in the hands of our President. If the people want to prosper, they must pray for and elect a President who brings them prosperity. Of course, this statement is made against the difficult background of the respect of the people's choice, without which the election exercise becomes a mere farce.

The point about the respect of the people's choice introduces the reflection on who the electorate think is a good president. African societies are still very ethnic bound; they are societies in which the tribe continues to exercise a decisive influence in everything we do and in the way we apprehend national issues. To most of us, a good President is anyone who comes from our tribe. Suitability is judged by tribal identity, not by any objective qualities that transcend those tribal considerations. And yet the search for a suitable national leader should prompt us to look beyond the immediate borders of our tribe. That is why the speech says in going to the polls nothing but our fatherland should be our guide. We should not vote for somebody simply because he is our tribesman. We should vote for him because he embodies the qualities that make for good leadership. If in addition to possessing these qualities such a person also happens to be our tribesman, then fine and good; after all, a leader must come from somewhere. But the destiny of the nation must not be sacrificed for tribal or even regional interests.

To dissimulate the tribal colour of leadership, people often point to the territorial spread of the party in power. It is true that such parties usually have some degree of national representation, but more often than not this representation is fictitious. Invariably, the core of the party, its heartbeat, is always situated inside the President's tribe. The rest of the people only comply or are forced to do so.

Incumbents who depend on coercion for survival develop a protective strategy that makes them dread the loss of power. Their fear of defeat is worsened by the horde of dependents battling to ensconce themselves further and more firmly in the system. The incumbent may want to concede defeat in an election, but since his departure means the end of privileges for his coterie of followers, they do everything in their powers, first to pre-empt such defeat and, failing that, to bend the election results the way of their President, that is to say their own way.

Uncertainty of post-presidential conditions is at the root of most African leaders' fear of democracy. It is clear that if they were assured a peaceful existence once they stepped down from power, they would be more willing, at least less obstructive, in their attitude to democracy. That is why in our maiden speech we made sure that the outgoing President was first of all thanked for his tenure and then given the necessary assurances of a quiet life in the event of defeat at the polls. If the choice is between the presidency and imprisonment, exile, or death, it is obvious that any right-thinking person will choose the presidency. The choice should be made more and more to lie between the presidency and a peaceful retirement in the full enjoyment of the prerogatives of a former Head of State. The after-me-the-deluge syndrome should be made to yield to a practice that puts the nation first and me last. For this new vision to take root, the political soil must be generously provided with the manure of justice, love and harmony. Once this is done, elections will be elections and citizens will no longer be passive spectators of their own destiny but full actors in the exciting experience of nation building.

The next speech I made was addressed to the youth and by all indications, this was the address that found the most favour with the public.

### The Youth

*I wish today to address myself more particularly to the youth of my country. I am a teacher and therefore in direct contact with the lives of the youth; a life made of ambitions and dreams, but also of legitimate hopes, which the State should hold as a duty to translate into reality.*

*Every teacher's dream is to see that the young men and women he has taught succeed. He is happiest when he sees that his products are in good jobs, in good homes, in good health. A country is mirrored in its youth!*

*We are in the habit of saying our country is a lion. This is true, but for some time now this lion has been like a lame duck. Such a bird does not resemble us. Our own lion is an animal in the full possession of its means, strong and gracious. To restore our lion to good health, we must first of all stem the shameful spectacle offered to us by our youth in front of foreign embassies in the nation's capital. Our sons and daughters are fleeing their country as one would flee from an epidemic. We need to restore their hope, urgently. They do not have another fatherland elsewhere. Their only fatherland is Cameroon! The children of Cameroon should not abandon the wealth of their country and go into an exile of misery and torture in other lands. Let me say this once and for all: the children of Cameroon are not homeless children! They have a home: Cameroon.*

*To talk of the youth is to talk of progress. And all of us know it: the secret of progress is hard work and honesty. Any Cameroonian worthy of the name must, from now hence, be hard working and honest. We must all roll up our sleeves and put Cameroon back on its feet. We must make the youth of our country the untiring workers on the site of nation building. That is all they ask from us and we will not let them down.*

**God bless you!**

Much to my surprise, the public reacted very warmly, in certain cases even very passionately, to this address. The positive reaction did not come from the target audience only; people of the older generation were even more effusive in their enthusiasm than one would have expected; maybe because by addressing the youth the speech had touched the family structure in the heart.

Youth employment is a crucial problem in Cameroon as it is all over the developing world. Education and professional training do not constitute gateways to jobs, as they should. Five, six years upon graduation or end of apprenticeship the qualified hands are still at home depending on their parents for their livelihood, where they are lucky enough to have parents able to provide for them. Because the local job market is non-existent, the nation's youth go to any length to seek hypothetical greener pastures elsewhere. The result is that foreign embassies and consular services in our country transform into refugee camps where beleaguered young men and women pitch camp night and day in the hope of a magical visa for Europe or America.

Strangely enough, this national calamity really does not seem to cause any concern at all. We even give the impression at times that we are happy to see our children go. This is one of the most difficult attitudes to comprehend, especially because nothing on the ground seems to justify the exodus. There is work to be done; there is skilled manpower to do the work; there is money enough to pay the manpower, and well. So where then is the missing link? Under normal circumstances, Cameroon should be a labour-importing country, very much like Switzerland in Europe, a country with which, by some strange coincidence, it shares some very striking similarities. Cameroon needs to come to grips with the paradox of is wretchedness amidst wealth. It is an urgent assignment.

The TV addresses focused each on a specific theme, a method that turned out to be very highly appreciated as many people came up to us to express their preferences and also to indicate topics they would have loved to see handled. The addresses are reproduced here-below as part of the way we view governance and social relations.

## Football

*It must be clear to us by now that the coming elections mark a turning point in the history of our country. Its main aim is to select from among the 16 candidates the one with the best promise of leadership, a person very akin to the captain of a football team. This is crucial. Like football, politics has its own requirements, especially when it comes to the very important business of leadership. Wealth, handsomeness, these are of little avail unless they are put in the service of good leadership. And a good leader is that person who sets the example, who teaches by precept. See him and you've seen his team. Watch him perform and you know what his team can do.*

*Football has brought us fame and glory. For that reason it is our most cherished sport. Our national team wins because each player is in his place. When we see captain Rigobert Song Bahanack, we feel good and certain of victory. All the players acknowledge him as their captain, and he has the makings of one.*

*The coming elections will give you the opportunity to choose a captain for the Cameroonian team of government. Choose correctly and you will be proud winners.*

## Crime

*Practically everyday in our towns and villages, crimes of one sort or the other are committed. Homes are burgled, pockets picked, human beings stabbed or shot. Even hospitals are looted. We live in permanent fear. But does our country deserve such treatment? This is the simple question I wish to put to those who take delight in such acts. When they make our cities and villages unsafe, when they make travelling a nightmare, when they warn off tourists and investors, how do they think they are serving their country?*

*Cameroon does not need crime. What we need now is a stable, attractive society that makes it possible for business and industry to* flourish. That's where the jobs are. Good jobs. Well-paying jobs. That's where the clean money is. That's how our country's reputation can best be preserved and promoted.

Cameroon's image has been very seriously damaged in recent times. That damage has not been inflicted by any one person. All of us take collective responsibility for it. Let us not forget that each time we do anything, however small, that is shameful, we damage the image of our country. And of all the things that we can do against our country, crime, in all its forms and sizes, remains the worst. We do not have much of a choice here if we want to forge ahead on the path of progress. Crime must go, and with it all its perpetrators.

### Hygiene and Sanitation

I wish today that we look at hygiene and sanitation. These are very important concepts, for they tell us something about our lifestyle; indeed about our character. You tell a man from his environment. If we tolerate physical dirt, we will equally well, and even more easily so, accommodate other forms of dirt, especially those that are not immediately visible but which are no less dangerous.

Hygiene and sanitation refer us quite naturally to cleanliness. And we know that cleanliness rests on three pillars, namely physical, moral and environmental. If we neglect any one of these pillars, the whole edifice of cleanliness crumbles. However beautiful or handsome we are, that beauty or handsomeness becomes an eyesore if our homes and streets are dirty. We therefore owe it to society to ensure that none of the three pillars is impaired.

There is beauty in cleanliness. A clean home is attractive. Clean streets are attractive. We always want to be where cleanliness is. It feels good being in a clean, flowered home; it feels equally good walking down a clean, tree-flanked boulevard.

But let's remember, cleanliness is not manna from heaven. It is the product of our own ways. If we litter, we will harvest dirt. If we empty heaps of refuse into our streets, we will harvest ugliness. Flowers are beautiful quite all right, but they do not sprout of themselves. We are not in the Garden of Eden. The flowers have to be planted and cared for. As we can see, cleanliness is not another *person's business. It is first of all our business. We are the custodians of our own environment.*

## Roads

*Let us look at our roads today. We all know that roads bring development and that without roads there cannot be any development. The final goal of the political game we are engaged in is the development of our country. The people need the conditions that provide for a normal, happy life. They therefore need good roads. The western world from which we take our examples know this all too well, that is why they do not joke when it comes to the state of their roads. They do not talk about their roads: they build them, everyday, everywhere, each one more beautiful than the other. They take care of their roads as one would take care of his jewellery, and the resulting beauty is breath-taking. Travelling in Europe is a pleasure. There you can live in Sombo and work in Yaounde or Douala, just as you can live in Mamfe and work in Kumba or Bamenda. Yaounde-Bertoua or Yaounde-Maroua become over there just a matter of a few hours' drive. That's what it means to live in a developed country. Our country is certainly not at that level yet, but it has the human and material means to get there. All we need is good vision and the strong will to lay lasting foundations; foundations that go beyond the egoisms of our fleeting present.*

*So long as we do not understand that roads are the most important development indicators, we will continue to mark time. And even after having understood it, so long as we will not get down to work, our country will continue to lose ground in this highly competitive world.*

## The economy

*The bedrock of social progress is economic growth. The good health of the economy depends on a certain number of factors, principal among which is government policy.*

*Conscious of the capital importance of the economy in the onward march of the country, the Social Liberal Congress has* designed a strategic plan capable of redeeming the country's ailing economy. This strategy operates in a calm social environment in which corruption, harassment and cheating are kept in check, if not eradicated altogether Our aim is to make Cameroon a choice destination for foreign investors and tourists.

Our economic recovery plan will rest on a free market economy that can attract capital mainly through such attractive policies as low taxes and customs tariffs, and minimum state intervention. This recovery plan will depend for its success on a good road and communications network that places our businessmen and women at the centre of the development effort.

## Women

*I wish today to talk to the women of Cameroun; that is to say, to my wives, my sisters, my loving mothers.*

*You make up a solid 51%, maybe 52% of the population of our national triangle. This strength of numbers makes of you the real custodians of our country's power. Don't forget: we are in a democracy; that is to say in the game of numbers. Your no is Cameroon's no; your yes the final word! You are therefore Cameroon.*

*This country is a thing of joy to you. You love it in a special way, and like all people who care, you want to see it cleaner, more beautiful, more dynamic, ever more prosperous. Your joy is in the fair manner in which the country's wealth is shared; your happiness is in that of your children.*

*But you ask these things quietly, gently, for such are your ways. You ask them because you care about the destiny of this country. You ask them because you want a better home for your children. You ask them because you want that the good things of life are made available to all. Cameroonians may not say it often enough, but they do not think it any less: you are the silent conscience of their country.*

*The world knows you for your beauty. This beauty is not only in your looks; it is especially in your ways. You will have noticed that the emblem of the Social Liberal Congress is a black horse.*

*That horse is beautiful. That horse is caring. Everyone calls it the Winning Horse. Do you still want to know who that horse is modelled after?*

## Crime

Let me ask you this question: who benefits from the mounting crime wave in our country? I ask this question because crime is so much at home with us that one would think we were its natural parents. There is never a day that we are not hit by crime, both in our towns and villages. So who then does all this benefit? Certainly not our country, otherwise we would not be complaining about it. Of what use then is a cause that is of no interest to Cameroon? For the only good cause I can think of is that which is of use to my country.

Crime does not pay. For this reason it should not exist. Head hunters, highway robbers, thieves and burglars, illicit traders, cheats and embezzlers, all of them should know that they are doing great harm to their country. They send away investors and tourists and jobs along with them. That is not all. They add to the general discontent by worsening the social climate. The country does not deserve this. We cannot seek progress by abetting disorder; we cannot seek social peace through murder and other crimes. This trend can and should be reversed.

At the end of the elections, Paul Biya was declared winner. In the spirit of democracy and sportsmanship, we immediately recognized his victory and wished him well while at the same time thanking God for having given us the chance to interact with our people in such an event as the presidential elections. The road is long, but we shall travel it, God willing. May all those countrymen who voted for us be thanked, as should the millions who saw in us a good servant and took a date.

www.ingramcontent.com/pod-product-compliance
Lightning Source LLC
Chambersburg PA
CBHW021131300426
44113CB00006B/383